RAMBLING TOWARD

TRUTH

Finding God in Beauty, Art,
Nature & Wanderlust

D. Whalen

Rambling Toward Truth is available on Amazon.com.
Please leave a review there to help spread this work.
The direct link is http://a.co/5yNuqJ2

For any person who is unable to consider how things originate, how they are led back to their end, and how God shines forth in them, is incapable of achieving true understanding.

—St. Bonaventure, *Lectures of Hexaemeron*

For all the Runaways, Ramblers & Truth Seekers

Contents

Introduction

Standing atop the Acropolis of Athens, as the moonlight refracted through the early morning dew of the olive trees, I was imagining how many had come here over the past 2500 years to see the iconic temple—the Parthenon, or to pay their respects to the goddess Athena. I stood there for several hours, unable to pull myself away, amidst a sea of thousands of tourists flowing up and down the hill. I was alone, though it felt good to be this way, as I could meditate without worrying about taking pictures or talking.

I began to imagine and reflect on all the hopes and desires of the billions of people who had lived on this planet since the beginning. I wondered how much had changed on earth in the past 2500 years since the Parthenon had been built. There had been billions born who were now dead. There had been zillions of desires, some fulfilled but most unfulfilled. There had been countless wars. There were saints and demons. All had come and gone. And there were many faiths, prophets, and gods: Athena, Moses, Mohammed, Jesus—the one I followed, and countless others.

In that moment of reflection, it seemed to me that all of history, all the desires of men, all the hopes, dreams, battles and joys, all was as nothing in the light of pure *being*—of existence itself, of just standing there. The beauty of the mind, its way of thinking, reasoning, imagining and creating, seemed the only thing of real importance, other than the earth directly under my feet and the air and sky all around me. It was the *now* that was important: the *now* of the moment but the *now* of all eternity as well. All that mattered was the recognition of being a *being* and of imagining my origin—my Creator.

I may have appeared to everyone on the sacred hill that day as being alone, and perhaps lost in myself, but in reality, I was with Another. I was walking with my Creator . . . in a different dimension. At that moment I had somehow detached myself from all the unfulfilled desires of my life, from all emotion and distraction, from my past and future. I just *was*.

I imagined that my favorite philosopher, Aristotle, had walked on the same ground that I was now walking on. Aristotle was one of the first philosophers known to history and, in fact, lived just a stone's throw from the Acropolis, born approximately one hundred years after the completion of the Parthenon. He had grappled with—and expounded on—similar musings of being, existence, and a Creator (known as *metaphysics*). I had come to love his writings over the years.

I am a sensitive person, perhaps overly so. I found that as I meditated on that hill, I was becoming distracted by hearing the thousands of somewhat mundane conversations all around me. Therefore, I placed a pair of hi-fidelity headphones on and began playing *Gjeilo: Song of the Universal*, performed by the Norwegian Trondheim Soloists. As I listened, my soul rose to an even higher state of transcendence. I was no longer standing there but now floating above the crowds, above all creation; I was in the arms of my Creator. My heart had never been so full of understanding. At that moment, at forty-seven years old, I had finally understood my entire life—past, present, and future.

Music has always been with me during the most profound changes in my life. Aristotle had written about the power of music in his work *Nicomachean Ethics*. In it, he argues that music has the dynamism to directly alter the very soul itself:

> . . . Anger and mildness, courage and modesty, and their contraries, as well as all other dispositions of the mind, are most naturally imitated by music and poetry; . . . for when we hear these our very soul is altered. . . . Music directly represents the passions of the soul. If one listens to the wrong kind of music, he will become the wrong kind of person.[1]

Aristotle admits that this applies in different ways to different persons. In some, such as the "fearful" or those "subdued by their passions," music can actually "overpower the soul."[2]

As you will see in reading the following pages, music has directly influenced my own life, both for the good and the bad. In my early life, it often led me to darkness, overpowering my malleable soul. Yet at this moment on the Parthenon, it led me to enlightenment and peace.

I became a Christian as a twenty-two-year-old. In the years following the events in this book, I began to think I needed to radically change myself through education and a purging of my past. I started spiritual direction where I was encouraged not to speak of my wild past as it would scare others away, especially in the pursuit of Christian marriage and a profession. I was encouraged to become an attorney. I was told that as a lawyer I would have power to influence the culture. I respected this advice. I began to read about St. Thomas More and imagined I could be like him—a lawyer, a married man, and a saint. Therefore I, a high school dropout, runaway, and former drug user, studied for years and eventually became an attorney. With the help of spiritual direction, I planned out my entire new life: I would be an influential professional, make plenty of money, get married to a beautiful woman, have several children, drive a Mercedes, live in a big home, and remain faithful to God.

I knew one day, after obtaining these desires, I would write my story of conversion. I had been writing since childhood—poetry mostly. I imagined being an attorney would keep me writing, so when I was ready to write my story, it would be well done. I always believed this was not so much my story, but God's story, and I owed him the telling of what he had done for me. But this would have to wait. First, I had to change myself dramatically if I wanted to achieve my goals. I would focus exclusively on professional life and creating a family and only after that would I write my story.

However, as the years piled on, my plans did not materialize. I became restless as a lawyer, I never married, and I rejected the seeking of money and material things as my primary goal. Instead, my love of adventure kept growing, and I began to travel all over the world, realizing a deeply held desire since childhood to *see the world.*

This created conflict in me, as I had been advised that my new faith required me to tame my adventurous wanderlust. I began to believe that once I fell in love, got married, and had children, my wandering spirit would subside and that I would find stability and put down roots.

But it wasn't to be. I would read spiritual books in the morning about St. Thomas More, but in the evening I'd read adventure books about Joshua Slocum and Amelia Earhart. I still wanted to stand on that mountaintop in a strange land, sail the high seas, or ride my motorcycle around the world.

Just a day before my visit to the Parthenon, I had been swimming in the Aegean Sea, in the same place that St. Paul had found himself shipwrecked. As I swam, I realized that I would likely had never been there had my hopes of domestic tranquility and stability been realized. I began to understand that I could no longer wait to be the person I hoped for, but instead I had to accept the person I in fact am. I had the profound realization that the life I now had was a result of actions I had chosen, even if unconsciously. There was only one path, and it's the one I chose, whether I liked it or not. It wasn't circumstances of bad luck: I wasn't rich, I wasn't an influential attorney, and I had no beautiful wife. But I came to understand at that moment that it must not have been truly what I wanted all those years. My subconscious mind had been acting against my conscious mind. I must have unconsciously wanted (no, I must have been born for) something else, something freer, something less materialistic, something more radical yet simple. God was speaking to me in my own actions, showing me who I was by what I had done, not by who I had wanted to be. The desires that had grown in me years after my conversion, even though I believed were for him, were not entirely the right ones. I had made a critical error. I had rejected my own identity out of envy and betrayed my own essence.

Now, I honestly began to trust God again, as I had when I first gave my heart to Jesus, without any hopes for betterment or desires for things or people. It was time to be me, not the me I had obsessively wanted or the one other's desired for me, but the me I had become. It was time to accept myself entirely as is. I was single and free with a wanderlust wild heart. God had brought me here just as I am. I was simply *being* with no disappointments or hopes—only alive and understanding.

But this person was not fully known to my conscious mind, as I had tried to be someone else for nearly twenty-five years as a Christian. I knew I had to explore this new man. I was confident that who I was now was inextricably tied to my old self, that person I was before giving my heart to God, that person who loved adventure, the purity of nature, and rambling about the earth.

One of my favorite New Testament passages is John 3:5 which says that *man is born anew in the Spirit.* Since becoming a Christian, I had relied on this passage to try to redefine my personality and my inner self. Yet now I was questioning, how do I reconcile this with the new understanding of myself? Who exactly am I supposed to be? Can I say that I am a different person today than the wild young man who lived before? Can I create a new man, liberated from my past? Can a person redefine who they are? Can a person truly change, as I had tried for so many years?

My trip to Athens inspired me to finally sit down and write this story as a sort of final reconciliation with God and the performance of my duties to him. But it was also a way to understand my past and to try to purify it for the present. It was to be a means to harmonize my entire life in one unity.

I dutifully began writing, putting much of my life on hold to finish this work. It has at times been exhilarating to relive my exciting and rambling past, but there have been excruciating moments in writing this book, having to face myself and quantify all the pain I have caused others and all the pain that has been part of my own life. Sometimes I felt like a lunatic writing this, presuming I could have some positive impact on others by telling my story. Yet I could hear my life's progenitor (as described in the following pages), that fictional character lost in dreams, Don Quixote, whispering to me, encouraging me to continue.

And now having finished this book, having revisited many of the places I have written of (and many of the memories), I have come to fully and happily accept that premonition I had on the Acropolis and in the Aegean Sea. I can now see God's hand in my past, and I cannot but thank him for who I was. I know now that not only my present but also my memory and my past—all together define my identity. I now realize that the past need not be an obstacle to my own growth and future. I am where my mind and feet have brought me, where I have brought myself. I have become what I think and act, not as I desire or want. I simply am. I will no longer hide my past or keep it to myself. I want to fully accept me for me, for my past, present, and future, and sanctify it all. I want to bring my past and present with me, finally dying in the state of grace and appearing before that great Beatific Vision of love and beauty, which will burn all sadness, tears, and pain away. Sometimes I am ashamed to have lived so disastrously as a young man, but I must be willing to give witness to what God has done for me and to be thankful that it was because of my wild past that God himself called me to him. He made me who I am. I was born this way.

Another underlying reason for not having written my story before was due to the idea of *discretion*, taught to me in spiritual direction. I spent eight years in school and tens of thousands of dollars to become a lawyer and dated countless women in hopes of finding a marriage partner. I can still hear discretion whispering in my ear: *the telling of your past life of dissipation will inhibit your professional life and make you less desirable as a partner in marriage.*

But as St. Paul exhorted, we must be "fools for the sake of Christ" (1 Corinthians 4:10). Therefore, perhaps discretion can at times be a cover for cowardice.

Fyodor Dostoevsky has several characters in his novels called *Holy Fools*. For example, there is Lizaveta Smerdyashchaya in *Brothers Karamazov*, who is known as *The Stinking One*: a homeless, penniless, shoeless woman who, while appearing the local idiot, is instead a beloved saint in her town. There are many Christians like her—who seem to many as total fools, and there are many people who could, in fact, accept this path in bettering their life. We should understand and even embrace this ideal.[3]

Today, in our society built on marketing and advocacy (instead of self-restraint and truth-seeking), there is much talk of winning, of being a winner, of finding success in all we do. This attitude is even preached in Christianity as the gospel of prosperity. But there are many losers in life who God holds close to his heart and who will be close to him in death, perhaps more so than the winners. This book is for them and for those with wild hearts and crazy imaginings.

For me, there is only one real goal in life, and that is to be with God upon death and to live eternity in heaven. Anyone can achieve this goal, even the homeless, prisoners, those who suffer psychologically, the wild at heart, the ramblers, and those addicted to drugs—the *Stinking Ones*. "God chose what is low and despised in the world . . ." (1 Corinthians 1:28). And he does this everywhere and to everyone, if we just listen.

My hope now does not require all the trappings of envy I grew to want over the past several years. Now my hope is far simpler: that I turn toward that Eternal Fount and never turn away. And it is my hope that you, dear reader, do the same.

1. Heritage

My father, Francis, came from a loving home just outside of New York City. His father, Francis I, had fought in World War I and was working in the insurance industry. His mother, Lillian, was a housewife. They were both practicing Catholics of Irish descent, though not extraordinarily devout. My father felt a vocation to the Catholic priesthood early in life. Therefore, he studied to become a priest at the Maryknoll Seminary in Chicago. However, as his seminarian studies progressed, he realized it was not his vocation and was asked to leave the seminary. He then joined the army.

My mother, Barbara, was raised in Grand Rapids, Michigan, by a Protestant mother and father who did not practice their religion. Her mother, Brandy, had mental illness much of her life and self-treated with lithium. Her father, Reed, was a banker and had done reasonably well for himself, being industrious and smart with money and the things of the world. Yet Reed and Brandy hated each other. When my mother was a child, her parents never spoke to one another. If information had to be passed, my mother would be their intermediary. Brandy and Reed stayed together only for the sake of their two children, my mother, and her brother Reed II. But the moment my mother became an adult, the two parents divorced. My mother did not grow up in a loving home, but it was a home that instilled in her the value of hard work. She studied to become a registered nurse and also joined the army as a young adult.

My mother and father met on an army base in Texas and were married within six months. At first, my father had tried to break away from her out of fear of commitment, having gotten out of the seminary not long before. But when he broke it off, my mother threatened suicide. My father later described to me that he was weak in making decisions and took her back out of fear that she would carry out her threat. He decided, too, that to be a man, he must make this decision to marry her, and so he did. My mother converted to the Catholic faith to marry my father. Formation included one talk with a local priest. That priest commented to my father that he didn't believe she agreed wholeheartedly. I think she did not convert out of a desire to live the faith, but only because she wanted to be married.

Over the course of the next ten years, the couple had six children. I was the fifth. I was born in Atlanta, Georgia, in 1969, and baptized at Christ the King

Cathedral (in a transept that now houses an adoration chapel). I was told later in life that I was an adventurous toddler who would try to escape from my crib by the novel use of blankets thrown over the rails.

My father found work in the insurance industry like his father. He was a responsible, loving father, but his heart was first and foremost attuned to the things of the spirit. Being a devout Catholic, he focused much of his attention on the things of God and the soul. Marriage and family life never changed this.

For example, in our living room my father hung a large painting of St. Anthony in the Desert, a monk living in a cave as a hermit, looking emaciated from his fasting and abstinence. In the painting, St. Anthony had a small writing desk, a crucifix, and candles for light. It was not a glorious image with its colors faded and its frame flimsy. Reflecting on this, I remember this painting as my father's primary didactic lesson for my life. I thought he wanted to instill in me that I would find happiness only in the abandonment of the world, in the embrace of Christ in the desert. The image had a certain romantic ruggedness, yet I did not want this life—I did not want to abandon the world.

This spirit of abandoning the world, which I later understood in the Latin as *contemptus mundi*, or contempt of the world, permeated my upbringing. I never wore new clothes: they were always hand-me-downs. Nothing in our house was new; perhaps this was due to poverty, but I often felt it was ideological. As one of my chores, I used to set the table with plastic dishes and cups. For my father, using the poorest instruments was detachment from the world—his life of St. Anthony in the modern world.

My mother, on the other hand, was much attuned to the material world. Everything around her was immaculately clean and tidy. She worked hard and loved the things of the world, like music and films, fashion, beauty, and art.

My mother's character was secular, which perhaps led her to misunderstand the particularly religious spirit of my father. I think she may have wanted my father to be more industrious like her own father, to move up in his job, earn more money, and provide more earthly comforts.

It is my opinion that my mother and father grew apart because of these differences. Soon, my mother became depressed and began to self-medicate. She wanted to move to Michigan to be closer to her mother, Brandy. My father accommodated, and my entire family moved to a small town named South

Lyon, located about fifty miles outside of Detroit. My father was able to transfer within his multi-state company.

My mother had only one brother growing up. Now she was the mother of six children who were all born just two years apart. She was living in a new home with no friends nearby. Her depression increased. Her personality was one of holding in her feelings, not talking about them, until a moment when the pressure would mount, and she would blow up. Finally, that moment came in our home on Lyon Boulevard. She attempted suicide by the taking of tranquilizers.

As a result, she was committed to a psychiatric ward. Her psychiatrist told my father that she had been the first patient he had known that did not want to return home. She enjoyed staying inside the facility, being able to express herself with the arts and crafts offered the patients there. The doctor emphatically stated to my father: "There is no way to save the marriage. Barbara does not want to be with you, and her mental health is not safe with you. You should not even try reconciliation."

When she was finally discharged, she wanted my father to leave the home. Initially, my father did not want to divorce her, but his anger grew when she asked him to leave the home, and he then filed for divorce. She was upset and did not expect it, even if her actions may be construed as natural precursors. She went to Grand Rapids to live with her mother. The courts granted my father full custody of the children. He would be the sole provider for many years—cooking, cleaning, and working full-time.

I was a toddler when these events took place, so my knowledge is limited to hearsay. As I became aware over the course of the next several years, I remember seeing my mother only occasionally. I was raised primarily by my father until I was ten years old.

My father was a good man, even if my other siblings and I felt he was overly religious. With six kids in a small house, we all shared bedrooms and ate simply, such as powdered milk and crockpot foods. He worked all day, but he would often take us to the beach in the summer after work and on weekends. We had fun adventures in the local parks and in Windsor, Canada.

Our family had a television, a small black and white one. We were allowed to watch some shows, but only if there were no romantic or sexual scenes. My father would keep his bedroom door open so that if he heard romantic music playing on the television, he would come in and turn it off. He didn't care for television and would lie down in bed and read religious books until falling asleep at 8 p.m. (to wake at 4 a.m.). He had a small twin bed with an old worn-out electric-heater blanket. Heater blankets were a way to save money; he would turn the thermostat down at night, which during winter would cause our breath to be visible.

One night, when I was about seven, he allowed the family to watch the television version of the film *The Exorcist*. Normally he did not allow movies, but he made an exception for this one. By the end, I was terrified and ran to my father's room. Crying, I asked him, "Could I ever be possessed by the devil?" I expected him to answer, *No, of course not,* and to hug me. But instead, he answered: "David, the devil is very powerful and can possess anyone. Normally it happens because the person allows him in by engaging in occult things. But once the devil possesses someone, God will not allow that person to do something against their will."

I was shocked that this could potentially happen to me. I never formed a specific decision to avoid the occult as a youth, but having seen this film and heard his words, I was sufficiently scared enough to avoid the things of evil. But I was not a religious person like my father. Instead, all of us kids made fun of his religiosity. He prayed an hour or more a day, went to mass every morning, and on Sunday would make us kids go to church. We all knew he had planned to be a priest before marrying our mother. We joked that he was obsessed with the Catholic Church. He only had praise for it and was critical of the rest of the world. He just liked to talk about saints, priests, and nuns. None of us children wanted to be this way. Once, when my oldest sibling Marie confided in him of her desire to become a flight attendant, he said, "That job is like being a trained monkey." His negativity on the things of the world was always evident and present.

Every night after dinner, my father would give us children a Bible lesson. He had an old thoroughly worn-out Bible—its bookends entirely frayed by overuse. He would ask one of us to read a passage, and then he would lead us in a discussion about it or would ask questions and make connections between readings. Now and then he would change the topic to science and would teach us about the planets. For me, those discussions were much more exciting than the Bible lessons, yet all of it would subconsciously mold me.

I began to see my mother more frequently as I got older. She continued to live with her mother but eventually stabilized and moved out on her own. Since she had been trained as a nurse before meeting my father, she quickly found a job and moved into an apartment in South Lyon to be closer to her children.

My mother never lacked employment opportunities as a nurse, and she changed jobs frequently, working in a psychiatric hospital for a time, in a nursery, and at all various types of nursing jobs. Therefore, she moved often—always getting bigger and better apartments and finally buying a house on her own. She showed ambition like her father and was able to continually climb the ladder of social mobility. After several years she had recovered from her psychological problems, never again having been known to suffer depression or attempt suicide.

Today, the majority opinion of the family is that postpartum depression had caused my mother's attempted suicide. She had too many children in such a short a time—six in ten years. She had not been raised in such a big family, so its demands were unknown to her. I think, too, that many in my family blame, whether right or wrong, my father's then overly dogmatic and critical practice of Catholicism.

After her suicide attempt, my mother stopped practicing Catholicism entirely and was never to return. She did not attend any church for most of the rest of her life. Her break may have been the catalyst for every one of her six children to begin to disregard Christianity and Catholicism, as she had done. Her fracture would undermine my father's attempt to instill in his children the faith he loved.

Eventually, my father was to request a Catholic annulment from my mother. It was granted on the basis that the marriage had not been entered into in full freedom. The tribunal held that while dating, my father felt pressured by my mother when she threatened suicide if he left her. The tribunal concluded that the vows were made under duress, and the marriage, therefore, had never been valid in the eyes of the Church.

The annulment, and my father's religiosity, created a resentment in me, my mother, and, I believe, in my siblings. Over time, I felt that my father lacked credibility. He considered himself a devout Catholic, one that supposedly did not accept divorce, yet it was he that initiated it. And how could it be that these two were married for ten years, had six children, and now some institution says that it was all a fraud? I (together with my siblings) mused that I was now considered a bastard since I was born out of wedlock. My father would continuously defend the annulment and affirm that we children were not bastards, but the idea was to stay in my own mind . . . and fester.

2. Early Childhood

As a young boy, I was sweet, peaceful, and had a humorous streak. I would continuously laugh and make jokes, so much that my family started to call me Lou, short for Lunatic, but in an affectionate, not clinical way. I never fought in elementary school as many other boys would. I was quiet in class yet silly at home. I was introverted among strangers, and would never speak out of turn, but gregarious among family and the few friends I had.

Growing up, we had a large field near our house, providing many hundreds of acres where we would play and have fun. I loved to roam and explore. But as I grew up I began to act out. I started to bust windows, steal, skip school, and lie. My father began to ground me regularly. I loved my freedom to roam, and now that was being taken away from me.

I was not a good compliant boy. I began to steal daily from whatever store I could and to smoke regularly during the day. Once, while smoking, I accidentally lit the woods near our home on fire. I burned down ten acres. I hid nearby as I watched the police and firefighters fight the blaze. I remember feeling the adrenaline rush through my heart and veins. It was a new, powerful, uncontrollable feeling. I was never found out.

But I would be found out for other bad behavior. Once my father was yelling at me for something I had done wrong, and I replied nastily to him. He then smacked me across the cheek.[4] But instead of whimpering as I would do when I was very young, I decided to escalate. I remembered him teaching us the Bible passage where his beloved Jesus taught it was better to turn the other cheek when offended. Immediately after he smacked me, I turned my other cheek, not in peace, but as a mocking religious provocation. It worked: he became infuriated and slapped my other cheek. I was doubly stung, but I felt like I won.

I have no reasonable answer as to where these vices of stealing, mockery, lying, disrespecting, and burning came from. I can only assume they were an unconscious acting out at a father I did not relate to, a mother who abandoned me, and a sense of finding excitement in danger and rebellion, a fallen nature.

As I grew older, and tired of being disciplined continuously (mostly by grounding for days or weeks at a time), I became aware that I had an option as to which parent I wanted to live with. Since I was finding so much trouble with my father, I decided to move in with my mother, who had since moved to

Virginia. This would be my first move but not my last. It was a benefit to having a broken home. I now had a choice of where to live.

3. Star City of the South

A few years after my mother's suicide attempt she decided to move away from Michigan. She got in her car and drove south, without any firm plan as to where she would settle. She eventually found Roanoke, Virginia, the Star City of the South, named after its lit-up star sitting atop Mill Mountain, overlooking the city. The Roanoke Star was erected in 1949 and is the world's largest man-made star, rising over a hundred feet. Its bright fluorescent lights can be seen from fifty miles away.

On the foot of Mill Mountain was the local hospital. As a nurse, my mother quickly found a job there in the premature baby nursery. She settled in and bought a house in the historic neighborhood of Old Southwest at the end of Allison Avenue. My youngest sister Elizabeth also lived there.

I was about ten years old when I arrived. My life with my mother started out well. She taught me different virtues than my father. Gone were the religious lessons and Sunday church. I never officially revoked my childhood Catholicism, but I had never chosen it, so it just was not mine to reject. I was happy to have nothing to do with it. In its place was my mother's extolling of the virtues of hard work and the achievement of goals. She taught that it was important I made my own way. She encouraged me to use her lawnmower to make money cutting the lawns of neighbors, and later she helped me get a job running model trains at the Heironimus department store.

I lived in the attic, a creative space with a pointed arch ceiling and a large Indian rug on a wooden floor. Artwork began to fill her new home. She particularly liked the artist Winslow Homer, adorning the walls with his bright outdoor vacation style paintings. The house was a bit run down when she bought it, but after a few years, she remodeled everything with her own hands. It became a beautiful, lively home. It engaged my little mind; I had never seen such art and beauty before. This was much different than my father's house: the sparse walls, one painting of St. Anthony, the dirty carpet and old plastic dishes. I never felt I had a home with my father—only a shelter where I slept and ate. His house was like a stark monastery, and hers like a bright sanctuary.

My mother started to feed me books to read. She gave me a book of surreal poems from Khalil Gibran entitled *The Prophet*. Gibran was born into a Maronite Christian family, later learning about Islam, and eventually becoming strongly connected to the Baha'i Faith. His poetry is a symbolic blending of all religion and spirituality. My mother liked the idea of a blending of religions, not being tied to any one.

My mind opened as I read its pages about dreams, work, love, the unity of all religions, and how the spirit can transcend the body and fly free. A mystical sense crept into my heart as I read and gazed at the accompanying ethereal artwork.

My mother encouraged me to write. She provided me with artistically illustrated writer's notebooks for me to jot down my thoughts and write poetry. I started scribbling down my ideas, even if I did not understand what I was writing. This seemed reasonable since the verse I was reading didn't always make sense to my unformed mind. My style was surreal, writing words in some order but not always having a specific meaning. I imagined that my mind moved my hand, which wrote what it wanted subconsciously.

Much unlike my father, my mother loved modern music and films. For example, there was always Cat Stevens or John Lennon records playing. I remember once when she and I were working together: I was helping steady the ladder she was standing on while she painted the ceiling. We were listening to the radio. All of the sudden it was announced that John Lennon had been shot and killed. My mother started crying, which in turn made me sad, and I too began to cry with her. I don't remember her ever having wept for her children, but music and films would make her emotional. My mother's artistically oriented tenderness drove my own tears.

Her favorite actress was Katherine Hepburn, who many would comment looked like my mother. As a child she had me watch films with her, like the nature-filled love story *The African Queen* and the adventurous *Butch Cassidy and the Sundance Kid*. In the latter, the two men were wanted in the U.S. for bank robbery and fled to Bolivia, which for them was a robber's paradise. I began to imagine that if my life were ever to get too much to bear, for example, if I wanted to commit suicide out of personal despair as my mother had attempted, that I would instead do what they did and flee to a poor out-of-the-way country. It would be my escape hatch from pain and trouble.

All of these new experiences were awakening in me an artistic side full of poetry, music, film, and art that I did not know I had.

4. Gender Identity

That first year with my mother in Roanoke was marked by peace, tranquility, and creativity. But I began to develop what could be called gender identity problems. I started stealing clothing from department stores, but it wasn't necessarily male clothing. I began to take women's clothing, even undergarments. I would try on items in the garment room, put on my own clothes over them, and shuffle out of the store. Later I would wear them in private.

I don't know why I bonded in this way with the things of women. I remember admiring my mother for her beauty, not sexually, but for her style and grace. She used to lay in the backyard in her bright, yellow bikini to get a tan, and I could see how beautiful she was. I had never really seen feminine beauty before because I had not lived with her until now. I thought women and their clothing reflected a softness and tenderness that I desired. Growing up, I did play baseball well—first baseman—but otherwise I was not a sports fanatic as many young boys of my age were. Instead, I had a newly growing thirst for fashion, beauty, and tenderness.

Why was it that I felt such an allure to the clothing of the opposite sex as opposed to my own? Why was my mind afflicted in this way? Or was this even an affliction? Looking back now, perhaps I began to identify with my mother whom I had never really known before. Maybe I wanted to emulate her.

This is not to say I was attracted to boys, however, as I was not. Even if, as an eleven-year-old, I did not kiss my first girlfriend Susan, who lived up the street, I always liked girls. This would not change, even if I could appreciate feminine style over bruteness in boys. My fascination and even identity with the feminine would only grow, and I would eventually become overly excited by their mystery to the point of glorifying them.

My early love for the feminine and music had a natural unifier at the time. I discovered the music of David Bowie, who at the time dressed in an androgynous way. His music, style, and lyrics had power over me. I would hang his posters in my room and listen to his song *Changes* repeatedly.

Experimenting with my own gender identity in the vein of Bowie's androgynism, I once dressed up like a glam rocker girl and walked around the city of Roanoke. I adorned myself in full female regalia: makeup, heels, and dress. I wanted to see what reaction I would get. I walked for several hours into the blighted and prostitute-filled downtown area. People yelled and jeered at me. The experience was a difficult one. I would never go that far again.

But I continued to be experiential in dress and appearance. For example, I would often wear a bright African Dashiki and walk the streets with a soured frown and my (growing) long hair. Just my passing by would scare others. I would hear the locking of car doors as I passed. This small sound made me feel unwanted by the ordinary world. I felt the fear of the world, even when I knew I was a non-violent person. Even today, I feel offended and unwanted when a fearful person locks their car door (or chirps their car alarm) while I'm walking by. I know they mean no harm, but it feels as if they are declaring: "You look like a threat to me."

As a young boy with an experimenting mind, I wanted to live in a world where glam rock, androgyny, and alternative dress and looks were allowed. I started to feel a strong opposition to the world of reality that seemed to reject me. I began to oppose social norms out of spite and out of hatred for those who didn't like me.

I quickly outgrew my androgynous style and love for women's clothing. I don't know why it came to my heart or why it disappeared. Perhaps I was not strong enough to stand up in a world that scolded me, or maybe I recognized my true nature—an ordinary boy but one with a sensitivity to art and beauty. No one was attempting to politicize my gender identity as is common today. There was only the music of Bowie. Everyone else was opposed.

5. Dreams of the World

Beyond this new artistic and even feminine side, an adventurous trait was developing in me.

I read an exciting tale called *Escape from Warsaw* by Ian Serraillier, a book about three children escaping Nazi occupation by fleeing across rooftops in Poland. As teenagers without parents, they were always in fear of being captured, and yet through ingenuity were to remain free and be reunited with their parents after the war. I felt an adrenaline rush just reading this book of escape and fear.

Around this time, too, my mother brought me to meet a lawyer who had a large, stately law office inside a historic home, full of stuffed animals that he had killed around the world on safaris. In his den were large elephant tusks, stuffed tigers, and elephant-feet footstools. My eyes began to open to the broader world, and I desired to want to travel as he. I was not impressed with the dead animals as much as I was of the locations of where he had killed them.

I soon developed an interest in people of different nationalities and heritages. I wanted to know others unlike me. Where this interest came from, I do not know. It felt innate.

I met a boy at my school, Tan Ngo, who was born in Vietnam and who became my best friend. We were both on the track team; I was the fastest and he the second fastest. He told me his gripping tale of coming to the United States as a refugee. His whole family had escaped in the middle of the night across the Vietnam border, running nearly twenty miles through the jungle. They then boarded a boat, packed full of refugees, and set sail for America. During the voyage, many would die of hunger and dehydration. One of the refugees had his arm bit off by a shark as he hung in sickness off the side of the boat.

His story, as well as the home of the lawyer and Serraillier's book, awakened in me a whirlwind desire of escape and adventure. I wanted this world to be real. So, I went out to find my own adventures. Just yards from our home was a large section of railroad tracks. Every day hopper cars full of coal would move through slowly. I would jump on and off the moving trains and ride them perpendicular to the caramel-colored Roanoke River. Sometimes I would ride them for miles and walk back home. It was an Eden for an adventurous youth:

the green trees, rushing river, mountains, and train tracks—all within striking distance of my home.

A strange and profound desire entered my mind when I was about twelve years old. It felt as if it came out of nowhere. I wanted to *see the world,* and I knew that someday I would. I still remember the precise location where I had this thought: on Walnut Avenue near my school. This idea did not come from my family since neither of my parents had ever been anywhere except a few states and border towns in Mexico and Canada. And yet I had this feeling. From where did it come? I now believe it was an idea planted in me by some higher force. This memory—this inception of an idea—would remain in my mind and grow stronger.

Around this time I had a dream that I still remember today as vividly as when I had it. I was hunting a deer with a rifle. The deer began to run and I to chase. I was a fast runner so was able to keep up with him. I chased him through a deep majestic forest, across rushing streams, and into great plains. All the beauty of the virgin forest was new and bright to my eyes. I cornered the deer and steadied the rifle for the kill. But just then the deer began to speak. He said, "Please don't shoot!" At that moment, I granted mercy to the deer and said, "How could I kill you after you had just shown me so much beauty of wild nature and imparted on me the thrill of running through it all? No! I thank you instead." This dream was as real as life itself and has stayed with me my entire life, influencing my views about nature, beauty, travel, farming, animals, and non-violence.

In that dream, my heart raced as a wild animal. In reality, I began to feel myself to be animal-like, and I had verification. I was a swift runner—faster than everyone I knew and everyone at my school. My vision was greater than 20/20. I had a heightened sense of my surroundings, even to a fault of needing to be aware of every angle. My hair was thick and full, growing extraordinarily fast. My reflexes rapid. God created my body this way, like a wild animal. I was ready to use it for adventure.

My hind legs were ready. Seeing the world, running, and escaping was to define my life for many years to come, even if I did not know it yet. On your mark, get set, go!

6. Brothers & Drugs

This new spirit of adventure had a restlessness about it. In two years, I went back to live with my father in Michigan. I missed my siblings and friends in the small town of South Lyon. But when I arrived, I was a much different person. I now had a ferocious appetite for music, poetry, and art and a disdain for the religion of my father. As soon as I arrived, my life began to tumble dramatically. My mother had never grounded me as she was hands-off when it came to parenting, but now it was back to trouble and grounding all over again, but this time with a new twist.

My sibling Russell was the closest to me in age. We had always been close growing up. I had missed him and was now able to be with him again. We shared the partially remodeled basement of our home. We both loved music so blasted it whenever we could. One of his favorites was The Who's *Baba O'Riley (Teenage Wasteland)*. Rock and Roll was pervasive in Detroit, earning it the nickname *Detroit Rock City*. Russell's life had changed in the two years I had been gone; it was no longer about exploring outside and going to the beach, but was now all about drug experimentation and rebellion. He would sneak out at night to party with his friends. He had made his choice to join the drug culture.

He began to disappear on long drug-fueled benders, which were full of criminal activity. He would run away from home often, staying at friends' houses to party. He was a ladies' man. The girls thought he looked like The Who's Roger Daltrey, and he had the same charisma—always having a girlfriend. He emitted confidence and coolness, and his popularity was wide. Everyone at school knew me as Russell's little brother, instead of as David.

Eventually, he was arrested. He and his friends robbed an old man of his possessions during a burglary and stole his car. They took the car out for a joyride, and a high-speed police chase ensued. During the chase, while high on drugs, they smashed the car and were arrested. Russell was sent to juvenile detention.

My two other brothers were also living there at the time. My oldest brother Francis III was not using drugs, but instead he was industrious, buying and selling cars for a profit. Once, as a thirteen-year-old, I took out one of his cars for a joy ride. I pushed it to eighty miles per hour down a local county road with a music tape playing in the car. I had discovered Pink Floyd and was playing *Run Like Hell* with its multitrack harmony, its chorus repeating the word "run" sixteen times, and its sound effects of car tires screeching. I felt that adrenaline rush again, and that desire for wild freedom burned in me. I took the car back home and parked it in the same place; no one ever found out.

My brother Patrick was also staying with us. He was using marijuana but avoiding the kind of drugs and trouble Russell was getting into. He kept busy with his friends and hobbies, one of which was dog breeding.

I remember vividly the first time I used marijuana. I was a young thirteen-year-old. Patrick, Russell, and I went under the porch of our house and lit up a joint. We also had some wine. It was odd how the buzz awakened my sex drive even though I was still prepubescent. I enjoyed the feeling it gave me.

Around this time, Patrick ran away from home. He, like my sister Marie had done a few years before, hitchhiked to Key West, Florida. The idea of running away seemed almost normal in my family. I wanted to go, too. Why not? I thought. I was tired of being grounded. At least I could start hitchhiking and get out of our small town of South Lyon.

7. Expanding & Exploring

I began to skip school and hitchhike to the Novi Mall, which was about ten miles from home. There I got my left ear pierced without my father's permission. There, too, I met a beautiful woman who worked at a commercial art gallery. I would sit glaring at her while she taught me about modern art. The gallery was full of lithographs by Joan Miró, who quickly became my favorite painter. She would show me that his art was a form of surrealism, the painting of the subconscious mind. I had already dabbled in surrealism, both in writing poems and drawings. I understood surrealism. She seemed impressed by my knowledge.

I then started to hitchhike to Ann Arbor, the home of the University of Michigan campus. I would go to the record stores and sit on the grass at the quad, observing the people. At that time, the quad was full of marijuana and drug use. Culture, art, and alternative lifestyles were something I experienced with my mother, but here it was more voluminous and tied to drugs.

When I wasn't skipping classes, I attended the South Lyon Middle School. There were two social groups at the time. There were the jocks and the burnouts, as they were called. The jocks were into sports and finishing school, and the burnouts were the dropout drug users. My brother Russell was considered a burnout, but I believed I was independent, trying to express my more artistic style. I didn't want to be in one group or the other. I resisted peer pressure. I wanted to be myself. I would walk around with my ear pierced and a shirt with a vertical flap to the side (like Luke Skywalker), which no one else had yet started to wear. I felt *avant-garde*. I didn't want to be a part of a group. I didn't care about popularity. I was a contrarian.

Drugs were readily available in South Lyon because of its proximity to the counterculture of Ann Arbor. I started to smoke marijuana often. I began to come home with bloodshot eyes, and my father took notice. He searched me and found a small bag of marijuana in my jacket. He knew Russell and Patrick had already been using marijuana for years, but disciplining them, or knowing the proper way to deal with them, was not something he had accomplished. But for me, it was different. He saw me going down the same path as my brothers and wanted to stop it immediately before it got worse.

8. Psychiatric Ward

To try to help me, my father put me in counseling. I didn't want that. I had begun to think marijuana was good for my artistic mind. I didn't fit in the world of the *good boy*. Ever since I had dressed up like a girl and walked the streets of Roanoke, there was a part of me that liked to shock normal society. I reveled in shocking my *goody two shoe* teachers and father. It was a dark gratification of manipulation.

I took this attitude into the counseling. The psychologist tried to question me about my early drug use, hitchhiking, and rebellion, but I wouldn't talk to her, so she had me take the Rorschach test. I played a game: I consciously set out to shock her by giving dark responses to the ink blots. I was fiercely independent in protecting the thoughts of my mind. What my father wanted from me, education and normality, and what I wanted for myself, exploration, art, and marijuana, were quickly diverging.

My game backfired. She said my answers led her to believe I was suicidal, and I was committed to a psychiatric ward. I exchanged my clothes for a hospital robe and moved into what looked like a ground-level hospital clinic in Pontiac, Michigan. There were typical medical machines about, sterilized floors, and rooms for patients. My room had a window overlooking the parking lot, giving me an outside look at the world. This view was tempting me to escape, but it was unbreakable glass and locked. The door also had a window, which was kept locked most of the day. The rest of the day was for doctor visits and community time. I shared my room with one other patient.

Several times a day the nurses would bring us medication to swallow. I had already experimented with drugs outside and was surprised I was fed mind- and mood-altering medicines inside. I had thought the point was to get me off drugs, not to give me more on a regular schedule. I learned from my roommate that the pills were much stronger if crushed and snorted. So instead of swallowing them, I started to keep the pills inside my cheek until the nurse left. I would then spit them out, and we would crush and snort them together, often mixing them with other pills to get a much bigger high.

My roommate was much darker than I was. I had a dark side, but it was contrarian to rules and religion, not anti-religious or dangerous. His dark side appeared more violent. He (like many in the facility) would listen to the music of Judas Priest and Ozzy Osbourne, continually quoting the lyrics about Satan in admiration. Instead of my life turning around in this facility, I felt that if I did not escape, it would become much darker very quickly.

I avoided involvement in the satanic talk and music. Perhaps this was because I had seen *The Exorcist* as a child. I wanted to extricate myself from that psychiatric ward as soon as possible because it felt like evil lived there. After a few weeks inside, I did just that.

One afternoon, the nurses moved us from the main building to an adjacent gymnasium to play basketball. My sharp eyes and awareness of my surroundings quickly located a door that appeared to lead directly outdoors. I immediately ran, slammed through the door, and was free!

Having daydreamed for a couple of years of running and escape—like that wild deer of my dreams—and having read the novel *Escape from Warsaw*, I was now ready to affect my first real escape only a few months after having moved back with my father. My desire for freedom and the adrenaline rush of running were to serve me in a practical way: to break me out of that teenage medical prison.

I had only light institutional clothes on, and it was winter, but I was able to hitchhike home, sneak into my basement room through the cellar window, and collect some clothing and other items for my first real run away from home.

9. Hitchhiking to Florida

I decided to hitchhike to Florida. At thirteen my facial hair had appeared, and I decided to let it grow out to hide my youthfulness. I was told I looked older and that I had a seriousness about me. I knew I needed street smarts now. My first ride brought me to the Florence Mall near Covington, Kentucky, where I took respite before continuing the southward trek down Highway 75.

I had barely any money, but I was an expert at stealing food from grocery stores. Rides would sometimes offer me something to eat. Sometimes they wanted something in return, but I would refuse them. One man put his hand on my leg while driving down the road. My heart raced fast, realizing the danger. Keeping my calm and afraid of escalation, I asked him to let me out at the next exit. Thankfully, he dropped me off without incident, but the entire time I was ready to jump out of the moving car at any moment. The only weapon I had was a small pocket knife. Would my gentle, artistic nature allow me to use it on someone? I didn't want to find out.

Somewhere in Tennessee, I got a ride from a man who was going to Louisiana. He was kind enough and bought me a meal. I noticed he carried a gun in his glove box, but I didn't have any foreboding feelings. I trusted my judgment. When we got to Mobile, Alabama, he offered that I could stay the night in his hotel on the second bed. There was no sexual activity. He was simply being charitable. Before he got too drunk and fell asleep, he made a point to tell me he sleeps with the gun under his pillow in case of intruders. Hours after he fell asleep, I proceeded to steal the money from his wallet he had left in his pants on the floor. I then fled in the dark of night. My heart was on fire with fear of him waking up and shooting me, but I acted quickly and efficiently. I didn't know about my guardian angel until later in life, but he was apparently looking over me, preventing harm from coming my way.

I continued to Florida by hitching east on Highway 10 through the panhandle. I got a ride to the intersection of the 10 and 75 freeways in north Florida. I arrived there late one night, but I was not tired, so I kept walking with my thumb up half-heartedly, not caring if I got a ride or not. A strange feeling of transcendence had come over me, much like what I had read in Kahlil Gibran's *The Prophet*. It was as if I had been transported to another dimension in time and space, free from my body. The colossal semis would fly by, each one creating an immense wave of air that refreshed and kept me cool, a spiritual wind. I continued walking for ten miles with my head in the sky, glaring at the bright stars above. I lost my youthfulness that night. There was happiness for finally feeling free to be me, but there was also an intense and mystical loneliness at the same time. The words of the Bob Dylan song *Like a Rolling Stone* came into my mind, and I started to belt them out at the top of my lungs, knowing full well no one heard me—only the universe above me and anyone who occupied that great space who bothered to listen.

I had been fascinated with running for a few years, and now it was entirely real. The wind on my face and the stars in my eyes. I was a *rolling stone.*

I remembered my siblings having told me about their hitchhiking experiences—how they would sleep on the side of the highways in forested areas. They warned me to beware of swamps, as there were many just off the shoulder of Florida highways. I had a blanket to sleep on and would rest right on the edge of wetland, not knowing how close I was to a swamp until the morning. I had a justifiable fear of alligators, as they were ever present in Florida, lurking about.

The next morning, I was picked up by a man who offered me a place to stay in Cocoa Beach on the Atlantic Coast. I had nowhere else to go. He had a lovely home, two floors with multiple sunlit rooms, and just a few blocks from the beach in a friendly neighborhood. For three nights I slept there, ate, and went to the beach often. On the third day, he made an unexpected advance. Before this, I didn't know he was homosexual. We were sitting on the floor, and he sat behind me, starting to massage my back. He asked, "Do you mind if I go further?" and I told him, "No, you can't." I had not had any sexual experiences to speak of and did not at all feel this was a good thing for me to do. He didn't force anything beyond that.

I didn't want to engage in that activity. I felt no attraction to men or boys. I had to get out of there. I had not thought through what I would do after getting free from home; would any thirteen-year-old have had a plan? I had nowhere to go and no money. My heart was now fearful after my two-week journey. I called my father, who sent money for me to take a Greyhound bus home.

10. Straight, Inc.

My father was now anxious about me: I had run away from home, I had been smoking marijuana, growing out my hair, and lying. I was only thirteen, and to him, my life was rapidly descending.

He decided to take drastic action—action he felt he had failed to take with Russell, who by now seemed hopelessly lost in drugs and crime. Russell was no longer attending school, was running wild, and was gone from home most of the time.

My father hatched a plan. He asked me if I wanted to go to Kings Island, an amusement park near Cincinnati, Ohio. It would be just the two of us. Of course, I wanted to go because the park contained the largest roller coaster in the world, *The Beast*. We got in the car one early morning and drove the few hours south. But we didn't go to Kings Island. Instead, he told me he couldn't continue to lie to me and was bringing me to a drug rehab called Straight, Inc. I reluctantly assented, not knowing what it was or even if I had a choice.

When we arrived, there was no marking outside the 10,000-square-foot building with its extended awnings covering its otherwise cinder-block construction. It lacked windows, looking like a warehouse. Once I entered the building, I was brought alone into a small five-by-ten-foot, cinder-block room. I was strip-searched, and after a long, harsh interview by several young men and boys, I was told I would be staying to be cured of my drug abuse. My father had disappeared the moment I entered the building, and I would not see him again for several weeks. Little did my thirteen-year-old mind understand that I would spend the next six months of my life in this rehab, which in reality was an aggressive and abusive cult.

Before going further, I feel the need to explain the program and its historical origins.

The Straight program was for boys and girls from age thirteen to twenty. In practice, it would take two or more years to complete. In the first phase of the program, the young member5 was completely controlled (much like a prisoner). Eventually, if the member went along, he or she would move up and gain more freedom. But even after graduating the program, the member would still have years of follow-up with a sponsor. The idea being that *once a druggie, always a druggie*.

The program was not run by drug treatment professionals; there were no psychologists or professionals of any kind. It was entirely peer and staff led. Kids who had gone through the program would become staff members leading the program. The idea was that this peer pressure would help the member to refrain from drugs, live a clean life, go back to school, and be productive members of society. There were no drugs of any kind in the facility (as there had been in the psychiatric ward); any and all drug use was considered abusive.

The defining philosophy of Straight was that even a thirteen-year-old who occasionally smoked marijuana and drank needed the program. It was not necessary that the youth was engaging in criminal activity; but if the youth was already using drugs, he or she eventually would become criminals if not treated right away.[6]

My father accepted this philosophy. Other parents and marketing material had convinced him I would die of an overdose if I didn't change.

There was no court order for this program: parents enrolled their children even if against their will. There was no outside entity or legal representative to assist the children. There was no one to call for help.

The program was not a charitable or government-run organization. Instead, it was a for-profit endeavor where parents paid a substantial fee. To earn profits, its staff members were trained in marketing, tasked with growing and expanding the program by bringing youth in.

Straight was founded by diplomat, businessman, and Republican political fundraiser, Mel Sembler, who was also a Jewish Reform devotee. Being well connected in the political world and knowing well the Reagan and later the Bush families, Straight grew fast. First Lady Nancy Reagan even visited one of the facilities, praising the methods, and also brought Princess Diana once, in turn improving its public relations and growth. Eventually, 50,000 youth had gone through Straight's doors.

Straight had several centers around the country. It started in Florida in the late 1970s but exploded in growth across the nation in the early 80s. The facility I entered in Cincinnati was new at the time.

Straight's origins, however, can be traced back to 1958, when Charles E. Dederich, Sr. founded the Synanon organization in Santa Monica, California. Dederich was an alcoholic who would become sober through the twelve-step program of Alcoholics Anonymous. Since AA was not oriented to drug use, he created a new seven-step program. At its core was something called Synanon Game, where drug users would go completely cold turkey from their drug and meet in groups to confess to one another things that they had done while on drugs, such as sex and crimes. The group would then aggressively critique the confessor if any ounce of the confession appeared inauthentic to anyone.

The differences between AA and Synanon were profound. Where AA holds that an individual must accept his alcoholism on his own terms, Synanon holds that druggies need to be confronted into accepting their addictions with drugs. In AA, there is no *back talk*, meaning whatever is shared by an individual is accepted by the group and no one is allowed to criticize; but with Synanon, the primary means was *attack therapy*, an aggressive, in-your-face confrontation, usually only seen in scared-straight, anti-prison programs or communist re-education camps.

The key to success for the Synanon organization was marketing, which attracted many famous people who would go through the program. However, the entire project devolved into chaos as some members were convicted of attempted murder, destruction of evidence, and terrorist activity. But because there was money involved, in the late 1970s the leaders tried to avoid paying taxes by reorganizing into a cult religion called the Church of Synanon. Finally, in 1991, the cult was disbanded following charges of tax evasion, fraud, and crimes against its members.

It is evident that Straight chose the Synanon philosophy as its core program, paralleling its seven steps, truth-telling, and violent attack therapy as its method of treatment. This truth-telling—attack therapy—was organized around what Straight called *rap sessions*. Every day from 9 a.m. to 9 p.m. (often much later into the night) there were dozens of these. The only breaks being for meals (even the meals were consumed in our same rap seats, balancing the trays on our laps).

A staff member would lead the rap session. This staff member would begin by speaking of his or her days as a drug user, and then would ask the group to relate to it. Members of the group would be invited to describe something similar he or she had done and explore his or her feelings about it.

In Cincinnati, we were a group of about one hundred, approximately sixty boys and forty girls. The boys were grouped on the left side of the room, and the girls on the right. We all sat in plastic chairs facing the staff member who sat on a high chair in front.

If you wanted to be called on to relate, you did not just raise your hand; you shook your arms violently. We were not allowed to stand unless called upon, but often our butts would come up out of the seat as we swung our arms. This was considered a Straight tradition called *motivating*. The staff wanted us to show enthusiasm. By the end of the session, the group's chairs would be moved chaotically about.

I refused to shake my arms when I first arrived, but the program was not voluntary. The druggie members next to me were asked to wave my arms for me. It was forced participation. But I soon discovered a benefit to motivating: it was very physical, and we would all sweat and get a workout doing it (filling the building with condensation and stench). There were no other means of exercise: no sports, no walks, no running, no outdoors, no nothing. There was a significant element of physical release to motivating, even if I did not want to be called upon.

Once called, the subject would stand up and relate. An ideal participation would include crying in front of everyone, going deep into facts and feelings of regret and pain. For example, a new member, called a *newcomer*, might admit having had sex with someone just to score drugs or having had sex with an animal. The member, however, could not blame others; he always had to relate what role he played in the fault. After relating, other members would then critique by shaking their arms, standing up, and aggressively confronting the person who had just spoken. It was *pro forma* that, if any of the others felt there was an inauthenticity about the share, they would then hurl brutal verbal attacks and insults at the person who just related.

There were twelve hours a day of this screaming of profanities and humiliations. It was all done in an attempt to shame newcomers into relating more accurately. It was mob rule by children: the *Lord of the Flies*. I recently read a memoir of one participant who described that she told her group in rap that her stepfather had raped her when she was thirteen. She imagined that the group would then understand where her problems arose and sympathize with her. Instead, the group blamed her for being flirtatious with him and for being a druggie slut, demanding she take full responsibility, refusing to give her sympathy or to seek professional assistance for her.

As in all things in life, some members learned how to cope: they would relate in such a way as to avoid any and all criticism. Many members would even lie, making up more dramatic stories to advance in the program without excessive attack critiques. The more you shared, the more freedom you would get and the sooner you would graduate. Criticizing in the group was also a way to advance faster. The members who criticized often would be praised by staff and would move up in the program quickly. Thus, there was an encouraged and inherent cycle of negativity.

There were five phases of the program. The newcomer was placed on the first phase, which generally lasted many months, and sometimes even years for the more rebellious. The goal of the first phase was to bring the newcomer to humble himself, realizing that he had a drug problem and had lost control of his life. There was no freedom of movement in this phase nor were first-phasers allowed to talk to parents, friends, or anyone in the program on the same phase.

I have since learned of one young man who spent nearly three years on the first phase, unwilling to participate in the program; all that time he was locked in and emotionally abused. As soon as he turned eighteen, he walked out. Within months he killed himself, believing he was a useless human being.

To prevent running away, I and everyone else on this phase was led around by the rear pants' belt loop. An *oldcomer*, a member on a higher phase, would grab the newcomer by the rear pants' loop inside a clenched fist and walk him to and from his seat. This also applied to bathroom breaks. If we needed to use the restroom, we would be led to and from it. Inside, the stall doors were removed, and the oldcomer would stand at attention in front of the open stall door. Having no freedom of movement meant there was no way to escape . . . just like a prison. If we ever sidestepped or acted in any way out of place, the oldcomer would put his knuckles into our spine to remind us who was in control. The oldcomers were the guardians and enforcers of the newcomers.

There were fights inside the building on a daily basis. If a member acted out or attempted to escape—called *copping out,* the other members would tackle him to the ground and sit on him—one person per limb and sometimes for hours at a time until his or her rebellious will was broken. If the person were extraordinarily rebellious, an extra member would sit on his stomach as well. This would often cause extreme agitation as the person would lose his breath (in my memory I can still hear the wheezing of others). People were also punched in the face and tackled; their skulls sometimes hitting the cement floor.

Violence was a way of life, a means to an end, the end being drug-free. I look back now with incredulity, but at the time my young mind only accepted what was a given. All I could do was try to avoid this abuse by not acting out.

At night we slept in the homes of parents who had children in the program. From the windowless facility to a locked car and from the car to the house, we would be led by the rear belt buckle by an oldcomer. Once a member reached the third phase, they could move home and be a guardian to other newcomers on lower phases.

When I first entered the program, I lived in the home of a local family who had a son in the fourth phase. He was doing well after a year in the program, attending high school. When I arrived at the home in the evening, the doors would be deadbolt locked from the outside (as per the rules of the program) so I could not escape. My movements were always guarded, including shower time. In the morning we would drive to the Straight facility by 7 a.m. Many of us would be locked in the smaller, cinder-block, windowless rooms, as we waited for the main hall to open for rap sessions. Once inside the main building, the doors were all guarded by oldcomers. This outpatient arrangement allowed Straight to bypass restrictive legal oversight laws that would otherwise apply to residential treatment programs. Straight was not a residential treatment program because the kids did not sleep in the building, and therefore Straight was not beholden to any regulatory body.

There was no school in the first two phases, but I did not mind this since I didn't like studying anyway. Instead, the entire day and week were about drugs, abuse, and raps. Most oldcomers ended up a grade or two behind, having been in the first phases long enough to have missed a year or more of school.

Going every day for several weeks as an impressionable teenager, I was eventually moved by some of the tearful stories. Some members showed remorse for the pain they had caused themselves, their parents, and others, even if some of it was fake. I began to accept that we were all broken children in need of help, even if my motivation was to avoid suffering abuse. It was impossible for me to continue to oppose the program for weeks at a time. I didn't want to be screamed at and sat on for months on end.

11. Escape

Even though I started to participate in order to gain my freedom, I still had reserved a portion of my inner-most self, not willing to spill everything in rap sessions. I always had eyes to escape. The group faced a long windowless wall, but on the sides were two large, fire-exit doors, which led directly outside. Each door was always guarded by members on higher phases. They opened from the inside by pushing on a bar, the reason a constant guard was needed. Due to fire codes, the doors could not legally be locked (otherwise, they would have been). Now and then someone would try to escape by running for them. It never worked. They would always be tackled or stopped by the member-guards, then sat on for several hours, and often beaten up.

I had been in the program for three months and had made it to the second phase. But one day during a rap session, I noticed one of the guards had left his post at the door for a minute. That wild heart in me beat hard; I could see as clear as day that deer of my dreams. My moment was now!

I jumped from my chair, and my hind legs flew toward the doors. I blasted through them as fast as I could. I was still a fast and confident runner, even if my legs had atrophied from sitting all day, every day. I kept running and quickly lost the kids who gave chase. I was free! It was my second escape from institutions. No one could hold me I mused.

Yet, I lacked a plan, again, as when I had run away from home. I had no money, and I was improperly dressed, having only a T-shirt and baggy pants without a belt, as per the requirements for students on the first two phases. I didn't know where I was, as I didn't know the area. I started to roam around a few miles away, but a local police officer spotted me, somehow knowing I was a Straight fugitive, and he immediately brought me back.

I was brought back inside in handcuffs, guarded by several members, and pulled forward by my hair to the front of the large rap room. The entire group jeered and screamed at me, hurling profanities: "You're a total loser, a druggie, giving a bad example, good for nothing; you *will* change your ways!" I kept completely silent. I buried my head in my hands—broken—my moment of freedom had vanished. They put me in one of the small cinder-block rooms for hours, a lesson in isolation. In these rooms, one could often hear other newcomers being beaten up and abused against their will.

I was the first person to have escaped from the Cincinnati Straight facility. After that, the doors were constantly guarded, and staff doubled down on blocking all the entries. Eventually, a large fence was built around the premises to keep members from breaking out.

Now I was back on the first phase and would be led around by my belt buckle again, being watched ever closer now. There would be two boys sitting, one on my right and one on my left, so I could not attempt escape again. I had to start all over. This time I knew the drill. If I did not share, I would be an unhappy and lonely prisoner. So, I quickly began sharing.

I made a secret deal with myself. I decided that I would allow myself to pursue the program authentically, but this did not mean I would agree to complete it fully. I would just do the best I could, and once I had freedom, I would then make whatever decision was appropriate, even if it meant completing, or running from, the program. In a way, it was a manipulation of my own mind to progress in the program, knowing that the only way would be doing so authentically since the other members could see through lies. I had to fool myself so as to deceive the others.

Thus, I shared because I had to, but I allowed it to become cathartic. Was I becoming brainwashed, or did I realize my helplessness to drugs? I don't know, but I began to cry and share about the pain in my life. I shook my arms wildly, shared often, cried, and, in fact, learned about myself. I did have regrets about what I had done: I had stolen often, smoked plenty of marijuana, ran away from home, and had early sexual experiences (though I was still a virgin). I admitted I had lost control of my life—all because of my problem with drugs. Now I would ask for help and was willing to humble myself. I was working the program but out of a deep and secret motivation of freedom.

I spent my fourteenth birthday in Straight. Now on my fifth month inside I finally made it to the third phase, where I gained more freedom. I was still not attending school full-time, but I was able to study some coursework. I still had to go to the facility every day but not for the entire day.

I was moved into the home of a single mother who had a son in the program, but he, being on the first phase, was not allowed to live with her. I now had the freedom to roam around the house and yard without an oldcomer holding on to me. The house was large and had an expansive view. The backyard ended with a cliff sloping down into a lightly forested area with a stream.

On higher phases, members were given duties; mine was to be the treasurer of the Sunday donation box. When families came on Sundays to visit the facility, a plate would be passed around, not unlike a church plate. (The only person who had ever come to visit me was my father.) The donations were used to buy donuts and coffee for the next weekend. I was given charge of guarding the box, bringing it to and from the Sunday gathering, and safeguarding it in my room at home.

On the third phase, I was allowed to listen to music again (as it was prohibited entirely on the earlier phases, as was reading and television). My mother, who expressed a distaste for the program, had mailed me a tape of Simon and Garfunkel's *Greatest Hits*. I would listen to it when I was alone in the back living room, glancing outside at the beautiful view of trees, stream, and sky. The song *America* brought a burning fire back into my heart. The lyrics spoke of going out to look for America on a ramble of sorts.

That secret negotiation I had made with myself after my first escape returned to my mind. I had convinced myself to use the program while I was there. This was for my own good—both to obtain freedom and to feel better about my life. But I don't believe I ever fully accepted the program in the deepest recess of my heart. My going along with the program was a survival mechanism instead of genuine change. What I wanted more than sobriety was freedom. This instinct in me had never gone away. It came to me as a pre-teen and lived intensely in my heart. I could still remember that moment on Walnut Avenue when that profound thought was conceived in my mind: that I wanted to *see the world*.

I knew if I stayed I would have at least six months left in the program and probably much longer. Some members were taken out early by their parents, and some pretended to be insane in order to be released into a psychiatric ward. I didn't want to go to another mental hospital, and my father would surely not take me out.

As I listened to Simon and Garfunkel, there was an image of freedom and happiness being painted before my eyes. But that imaginary painting had to become real. And so it would be. I took the money box I had custody of, slid open the large glass patio door I would often look through daydreaming, and I walked out . . . into freedom. I rolled down the steep hill to the forested area near the stream below the house and cracked open the money box where I happily discovered fifty dollars. I was free . . . after six months! This time I had money to effectuate an escape. I had a plan and the means.

I made my way to the Greyhound bus station. There, I bought a ticket and a pack of cigarettes (mimicking the song). While waiting I hid outside the station and in crevices inside, fearing Straight staff or police would know where to find me. Finally, the bus was ready to load. I walked aboard, holding my head high with a fast beating heart and my head swimming with Simon and Garfunkel lyrics of boarding Greyhounds and traveling through America.

12. Sex & Guns

The bus wound its way through the rolling hills of Kentucky and the wild and wonderful West Virginia as it made its way to Roanoke. I had the belief that my mother would take me back in since in her letters to me she had expressed displeasure with the Straight program. I believed she wanted me to live with her again. I was correct. She took me in upon my arrival. My father was upset, but apparently, there was nothing he could do. The two must have made some compromise.

I was happy to be back with her. She had moved into a larger three-story home in the neighborhood of Grandin Village on Westover Avenue, and she was remodeling it as was her hobby. When I arrived, it was already a warm and inviting home, full of artwork, music, plants, and many animals. She had built an entire walk-in, screened, upper-level porch that was for the exclusive use of several birds: yellow and greenfinches, two cockatoos, and several other beautiful birds. She also had a full-blooded sheepdog, a border collie, and a Yorkshire terrier. There was a cat as well.

Her home was alive with art. Some of the paintings on the walls were created by her brother Reed, who had spent his entire life as a starving artist in Chicago (though he sold enough of his artwork to survive). And there were sculptures everywhere. She had begun to sculpt small clay figurines of imaginative and deeply expressive human busts, placing them around the house. One of them reminded me of the famous *Scream* painting by the Expressionist artist Edvard Munch.

It was as if there was so much creativity in the home that it was impossible to see and feel every piece of beauty and knowledge therein. There were dozens of classical books of literature as well as books full of reproduced images of famous artwork. I would scour them. After a while, I could name an artist by looking at his or her art, even if I had never seen that particular piece: *Oh yes, that is Monet.*

I was fascinated with the art books. I could see patterns and styles quickly, even though I had no talent for painting. Many of the art books showed the natural beauty of the naked human body. This would have been prohibited in my father's home. As a young man nearing fifteen years of age, these inflamed my passions and imagination.

My mother was not always watching me as my father had. She gave me more freedom partly because she usually worked nights and slept during the day. Her primary concern was that I got a job and not present her with any trouble. Therefore, I started working, flipping pizzas at the local Tanglewood Mall. It was there that I would have my first sexual experience, which was not of love but of using a woman (the mall's janitor) for pleasure. She was over eighteen and therefore breaking the law since I was a minor. I feel shame that my first was not a girlfriend or someone I loved, but instead, simply a means to an end. And I too was merely a means for her. My judgment was clouded by my years of bad decisions, risky behavior, loneliness, and marijuana use. There existed in my heart a loneliness and a desire to express my sexuality.

I started to make friends in the neighborhood, at school, and in my job. Everyone I met was smoking marijuana. Therefore, all of my friendships were focused on getting high. I did not want to be sober and drug-free. Drugs were everywhere. Straight was just a blip on the radar for me. Their method of using force for sobriety did not affect me.

Roanoke is within the land of Dixie. I was a carpetbagger from the north (as was my mother), but all of my new friends had been born in the South. I did not have the southern drawl as they all had, but I quickly learned and would just as easily use the term *Y'all* as they would.

The Dixie flag was prevalent everywhere. Since my early childhood, I had never understood or accepted racism. But, in general, Dixie did not appear to be about slavery or racism to me as blacks and whites intermingled more than I had seen in the north. Some of my friends had the Dixie flags in their rooms, and some even painted it on their cars, like the *Dukes of Hazzard* had popularized, but I never experienced any overt racism among my friends.

My first friend in Roanoke was Mark, who became my best friend. I called him *Freebird,* and he called me *Kickass Dave.* I was the kid from Detroit who wore Bob Dylan buttons on his jacket, and he was the southern bred fan of Lynyrd Skynyrd. He lived in a large house with his brother and mother. We smoked marijuana in his room. His mother turned a blind eye, refusing to discipline him. She was a pretty woman, and I thought she was very friendly since she never chided our bad behavior as long as we kept reasonably quiet.

Mark and I both liked cars. He owned a 1970 Chevy Chevelle SS, with a modified four-barrel carburetor, light-green paint job, and large mag wheels.

It was a fast car—a real hot rod. Mark spent the majority of his time working on it. Once he and I were driving around, getting high, and I had a toy water gun that from a distance looked like a real handgun. As he drove, I waved it around at passing cars to scare people. We laughed hilariously at the expressions of total fear by passersby: "Look at that idiot!" Mark would cry, and I said, "Yea, what a fool!" It was just a silly game, played by a couple of young stoners. I would never harm anyone, but I loved jokes and having fun.

Suddenly, as we exited the local McDonald's and began to pull back onto the road, we first saw one cop car to the north, then one to the south, and then several more coming in every direction. They surrounded us with their lights flashing. We pulled over, and the police immediately opened the driver side door, throwing Mark to the ground. As they pointed their guns directly at me, they yelled, "Put your hands in the air and get out of the car!" Having no idea what it was about, I was scared to death, never having had weapons pointed at me before. I thought we were being busted for the marijuana we had. But Mark had quickly eaten it as we were pulled over.

We were both handcuffed. One officer yelled out, "We have it!" picking up the plastic water gun. Then another police cruiser came rolling up with two people in the back seat, a child and his mother. The child identified me as the person who pointed a gun at him. He had been so frightened by my waving the gun that his mother called the police to report me. They had thought it was a real gun. They decided to press charges against me. I was arrested for *brandishing a firearm* and booked into juvenile detention.

I had been home with my mother for about a year since escaping Straight, and she was now distraught with me. Unbeknownst to me, she had told my father, who then proceeded to drive to Roanoke to bring me back to Straight. But I spotted him in his car as I was walking home one day. He had two young men with him, who I found out later were both members (on higher phases) of the Straight program. Straight had a history of notorious kidnappings. When I spotted them, they also spotted me, and the two jumped out of his car and gave chase. But because I was so fast a runner, I was able to disappear into a nearby field of sunflowers.

I wasn't going back to Straight, and now I knew I could not go back to my mother's home. So, I ran away again. Run, David, run! Everywhere I was to run.

13. St. Petersburg Independence

My parents put out warrants on me as a runaway. I was fifteen and not emancipated. I heard that a family friend from Michigan moved to Florida. His name was James (but we called him Fat Boy). He was two years older than me and had been close to my brother Russell. By phone, he invited me to come south to St. Petersburg, Florida, where he now lived. He was working there as a fence installer with his father.

So, I hitchhiked to Florida again. James allowed me to stay in his home a few days and helped me to get a job at the fence company. With my first paycheck, I was able to rent a small monthly room in a roach motel in downtown St. Petersburg. The room was the length of a twin bed, and its width only double that of the bed. Inside it had just the bed, a small toaster oven, and a mini-fridge. There were so many cockroaches that I once put one inside the toaster oven to explode it as an example to the other roaches. It worked, they all fled! But, of course, they came right back in the dozens.

I worked with James for a few weeks while I saved money. I bought a V8 Chevy Impala for $400 since only five of the eight cylinders were firing, but it ran and provided me with the ability to get around. I didn't have a Florida license and didn't bother to register the vehicle, insure it, or get tags for it.

Having a car provided me the opportunity to find better employment. I found a decent paying job selling tools at a flea market, located about a thirty-minute drive from my hotel. The owner, Mr. Tembrillo, was selling all kinds of power tools and high-end American-made socket sets, like Matco and Snap-on. He was a kind and fair man and wanted to help me. He gave me independence to work by myself. But the temptation was too much for me; when alone I started to steal from the cash register . . . substantially. I was primarily earning two salaries: one from Mr. Tembrillo and the other from theft. He didn't know because he had no system for tracking inventory. The customers were happy since I was selling specific items to them cheaper to pocket the money quicker.

I didn't spend much time in my hotel since it was dirty, small, and the other residents were drunks and drug addicts. The common area was depressing: the residents sat around watching television, smoking, and drinking. I was not a bum and didn't want to be one. I felt out of place.

At nights, I would walk a few blocks to the oddly-styled, inverted-pyramid St. Petersburg Pier[7], to drink beers, smoke, and watch fishermen. One evening an attractive woman who lived on a boat in the attached harbor asked me, "Do you want to come on my boat for sex?" I told her, "Yes, of course," as she was gorgeous, but she then said, "My husband will be joining us there." "Absolutely not," I told her. I had no desire for this; I'm only glad she told me before I wandered inside. I never had homosexual relations or desires for strange sexual behavior like this.

But everywhere I went there seemed to be perverted people wanting to use me sexually. Looking back now, these adults were attempting to have sex with a minor. They could have been arrested. But back then I was a fugitive runaway, and the thought of turning people into the police would not have even occurred to me. For me, contacting the police meant going back to Straight.

Some days after this I was driving my Impala from work, and the police pulled behind me, flashing their lights. I was scared to death but pulled over. Luckily, they didn't know I had a warrant by my parents as a runaway, and I was only cited for driving without a license, tags, or registration. They impounded my car, and I was given a summons to appear in court. I had to walk back to the hotel. I now had no transportation to get to work, so I lost my job. My friend James could no longer help me. I had nowhere to go again, so I went back to Virginia in the hope I could somehow convince my mother to take me back in.

I never went to court or took any action on the summons. I just left. This would come back to haunt me later. I had lived in St. Petersburg on my own for several months.

14. Graveyard Spirituality

I went back to Roanoke and slept at various friends' houses while I tried to convince my mother to let me return. She finally relented. She took me back after I promised her I would be better—working, going to school, and staying out of trouble. I knew my mother was pliable and susceptible to promises of me changing. But it wasn't pure manipulation: I was more mature now; my living independently in St. Petersburg had helped me. I didn't want to go back into a roach motel with bums as my neighbors. I needed to be more careful and cautious. Of course, I had not given up marijuana, but I needed to hide it better and avoid any legal trouble.

My mother and I bonded well again. She liked having a young man around to help with the more physical aspects of remodeling her home. Much of the interior renovation was complete. She had stripped the stairs and all the floors to their original hardwood state and then stained them all. Every single room had been painted a different bright color with wallpaper trim, leaving each room with a feel of royalty. She did this all herself with the help of her children.

She wanted me to help paint the outside of the three-story house and to landscape the entire lot. I first got to work painting under her direction. The whole exterior was painted a pale yellow. I then went on to dig large holes in the backyard, planting various kinds of pines and exotic trees. In the front yard, we planted an intricate garden of numerous flowers and plants, twenty-some different varieties in a small space. She wanted almost every inch of her property to be full of plants. Her gardening was always well done, but I could see an obsessiveness in her plans; she seemed never to want to stop—there was always more. I gained a green thumb under her tutelage. I loved this work outside, creating and refining nature and the home. When she finally moved out years later, the entire front yard had become a massive, weed-infested mess, as the new owner failed to continue the substantial upkeep of caring for the intricate garden.

During this time I was going to school and doing the bare minimum to avoid trouble. I began to spend much of my free time in the nearby Evergreen Cemetery with its fifty acres of well-groomed grass, towering trees, dozens of large sepulchers, and thousands of graves. Some of the tombstones reached back a century. The cemetery was founded in 1916 and before that was known as the *Old Solitude Farm*. It was a peaceful place for me to spend time. It is where I learned the art of meditation. I would go alone, smoke marijuana lying in its grass, look at its trees for hours, and listen to the birds chirping and the wind softly blowing through.

While sitting there in a meditative state, there were times when I would *see* the trees, see their essence so to speak. It is hard to describe the sensation: it is as if the underbelly of the leaves would flip over, swaying in the wind, presenting a shade or shadow of reality. I would watch the tree flow, not as a part of just nature, but as something almost divine and spiritual. *Seeing* in this way did not happen all the time, but I was always happy when it did. Sometimes today I can see in this way, though less frequently; it is a spiritual moment for me to perceive a tree's essence like this. The only prerequisite seems to be a light breeze and a heightened internal sense of the mystical.

I would often jump the fence in the morning before it opened and sit admiring the large glorious trees in the early morning dew, writing and meditating. Over the years, I have kept some of my earliest attempts at writing. Here is one of the *surreal* poems I wrote there:

> *Hop the fence into the graveyard;*
> *Once you're in, not a way out.*
> *You keep worrying, keep worrying,*
> *On those nights the full moon is out.*
> *You walk the lanes of tombs,*
> *In star-crossed circles,*
> *And watch as the trees grow old.*
> *Now I understand that I'm just in circles,*
> *And time is no more.*

A spiritual love of nature began to grow in me on the Old Solitude Farm. It was there that I started to love the earth passionately. Not only did I fall in love with nature there, but nature began to present my mind with questions. As I looked at the trees in deep meditation, I began to reflect on the *why* of a tree. What is it and *why* is it? This was my first peek into the divine question of *who is the Creator.*

When I first moved in with my mother five years before on Allison Avenue, she had me plant four pine trees in our backyard. I went back there from time to time to see how the trees were doing. They had all grown tremendously fast. The small two-foot seedlings I planted were ten feet tall now, bushy and beautiful.

Sitting in the graveyard, I began to deeply reflect on the growth and life of trees: a seed is dropped from its branches and rainwater and sun help the seedling to grow. Then the entire process starts all over again—a constant cycle of growth and rebirth, all fueled from the soil, the earth, rain, and the sun.

What made me most curious was the very first seed of the very first tree. Where did it come from? Where did the first seed on earth come from? How could a tree just evolve out of nothing? Did a Creator create the first seed? It was the only reasonable explanation.

Although I hadn't practiced religion since leaving my father and his faith, I never disbelieved in a Creator. I just didn't know who it was and did not believe it was the God of organized religion, particularly not the overly dogmatic Catholic God of my father. But now I was relatively sure there was, in fact, some Creator, something or someone that had begun the entire natural process.

Once I let my friend Mark draw a picture in my poetry notebook. Next to my surreal scribblings and poems, he drew an upside-down cross with a grim reaper. Many of my friends had these satanic styled ideas, mostly from the popularized music of the time. I stayed away from this. My mind became attuned to some sort of good Creator, not a hateful destroyer the satanic music and imagery depicted. Even in the graveyard, there were signs of Satan. There were some sepulchers with broken glass and broomsticks thrown inside. There was a rumor that there were witches in the area. There is a city next to Roanoke called Salem, generating suspicious legends and tales. I would use drugs with my friends and listen to rock music, but I would never participate in their more cultish activities or listen to their satanic music. I would always walk away from that.

God was protecting me from myself and evil, and nature was now showing me a good and creating God. The graveyard was my peace. I often muse (even though I have not lived in Roanoke for thirty years) that when I die, I want to be buried there in the Evergreen Cemetery.

15. LSD & Evil

By then I was smoking marijuana daily. I loved the idea of marijuana—how it grew from the ground. A unique plant I thought, given by the Creator, raised from the soil, aiding my poetic creativity and the expansion of my mind. The only problem was having to pay for it.

One way was to steal from my mother's purse, which I did often. She never noticed, or perhaps she did but didn't want to say. I knew that she would often turn a blind eye to me. But this money was not enough. I needed more. The logical conclusion was to grow my own marijuana plant. I now had a green thumb after all. I saved seed from one of the better strains of marijuana I had bought, which had been moist and full of tetrahydrocannabinol (THC), having a bright green and purple color. I planted the seed in a tiny cup in my room at home. I lived on the third floor, and my window faced the southern sky without a tree impeding the sun's rays. I placed the cup on the window sill. It was innocuous as it grew. My mother had small plants all throughout the house, so when it started to grow, it was not particularly out of place. She did not know what a marijuana plant looked like. She never used drugs or alcohol. Her entire annual alcohol intake was only two fingers of wine at Christmas. As the plant grew larger, it became conspicuous, since it was a weed, not a houseplant. But since my mother often worked the night shift and would sleep during the day, I could leave the plant inside near the window during the sun's hours. The days she was home, I would hide it behind the chimney on the roof, where it still received plenty of sun. Finally, the plant grew so large—two feet tall—that I had to move it to a field near the house, behind the Mick-or-Mack store. As I fed it plant food, it continued its rapid growth, growing nearly four feet tall. But just as its large, bright colored buds started to come out, the plant disappeared. Someone must have seen me attending it and stole it. I never got to smoke the buds, but growing it had been a significant experiment for me.

LSD was another drug I began to experiment with. It would play tricks on my mind; sometimes I would see and listen to trees talking to me. Everything was a swirl of color, and the shapes of things would bend and sway when they usually were solid. Strange people would appear as if ghostly images in my mind and then disappear. I enjoyed smoking marijuana, either alone or with friends, but I would use LSD only together with others. It was just too dangerous to use alone. I did use it alone once, at a Grateful Dead concert, but it scared me; it felt like I was trapped in a gerbil cage with thousands of mentally defective people trying to sell things and engaging in perversion—all while police were looking on.

Often a group of us would plan an activity while tripping, like watching the film *Pink Floyd: The Wall*. I would eventually know every word to that entire powerful soundtrack, including its sound effects of ominous plane crashes, babies crying, and foreboding helicopters. The lyrics have stayed in my mind since then. Usually, we would take the hits at night and then stay up until morning. It was impossible to sleep for at least eight hours after taking LSD. It was something we would do around once a month, unlike daily marijuana use.

Over time, LSD directly affected my psyche. I've since seen family photos of my lovely, smiling, and innocent nieces, sitting next to me during this time. I wore strange rock and leather jewelry, and I no longer smiled but now peered from my dark eyes into darkness. I appear as a brooding, long-haired, open-shirted, hairy-chested soul, full of dark mysticism, dabbling both in the light and dark.

Everyone said LSD expanded one's mind, and it seemed real to me. Yet all of my experimentation and drug use presented dangers as well—mostly in the various oddball characters who sold or abused drugs. One youth my age, in my circle of friends, was Robbie May. He lived nearby on Mountain View Terrace. He always had marijuana and other drugs for sale: LSD, hash, and even crack, which I tried for the first time with him. Though I never liked going into Robbie's house, I often had to in order to obtain drugs. Whenever I did go inside, I felt an evil presence there. His home sat on a small hill. Walking up through the unkempt lawn, with its wild overgrown trees, felt like something out of a horror film. His parents did not control his bad activity. I knew he had been arrested multiple times for various offenses, but he always got away free, as he was a minor like me. After a while, I no longer wanted to go inside his home. My friend Mark would go in, but I preferred to wait in the car. Sometimes Robbie wanted to hang out with us as well, but I would always avoid him. I felt I had an attuned intuition and knew he was trouble.

It wasn't long after, that tragedy struck. A few years after I left Roanoke, on one single night, Robbie May was to murder two women and three men in cold blood—some of whom were good friends of Mark. It was a New Year's Eve,

Robbie had gotten drunk and was probably high on LSD. He stole a friend's gun and went to a neighbor's party. Inside their apartment he got into an argument, which according to a mutual friend of ours had to do with the military; apparently, some of the men there had been Marines, and Robbie, being a nobody, a handy-man, and drug dealer, was upset by their being in the military. With the stolen gun Robbie shot two women dead while they slept, and the three men he forced face-down onto the floor and shot them. All five were shot in the head, execution style.[8] His motive was unclear, but he was out of his mind—most likely extremely high. It happened on King George Avenue in Old Southwest, just a few blocks from my mother's first home on Allison Avenue.

Today, Robbie sits in prison for life at the Buckingham Correctional Center in the tiny town of Dillwyn, Virginia. He would have been given the death penalty, but for a psychiatrist who testified that Robbie had borderline personality disorder since the age of five. In elementary school, Robbie started biting his arm from wrist to shoulder, and throughout his teen years, he would cut himself.[9] I remember his arms—so violently cut up. In his teen years, when I knew Robbie, he attacked his relatives, including his own mother, who he once picked up and threw violently across the room. I remember the times I went into his home, feeling a deep despair and fear—a total cruelty and lack of love in the home. Before the massacre, he had been convicted some thirty times for various crimes of larceny and assault and had been committed twice to psychiatric facilities. Sadly and tragically, my intuition about him turned out to be correct.

In all truth, I would like to see him again and have recently attempted to visit him without luck. I wish him true reform and even happiness. I personally and firmly oppose the death penalty, but I do accept that perhaps only confinement and control can provide one such as him with the ability to live a long and meaningful life.

Despite all of my own drug use and poor choice of friends, I kept the peace at home with my mother, hiding all of my wild behavior and friends from her. Yes, she turned a blind eye for the sake of harmony, hoping that I would mature as I aged. It was her way—her style—to feign ignorance, keeping her eyes only forward, not on the insanity caused around her by myself and others.

16. European Dreams

During this time I continued to attend some school classes, but not all, and was able to eke by for a year. I had no plans for my life. I enjoyed poetry, art, marijuana, LSD, earthly meditation, and, of course, music. But I was not violent and was not committing crimes as many of my friends were.

My mind began spiritualizing everything. I remember sitting on the hill above my school one afternoon. I skipped classes and smoked marijuana while listening to John Lennon's song *Watching the Wheels*. I just sat there and watched the world pass by—the cars and people rolling on. It was a seminal moment in my life. Watching, observing, and spiritualizing the world through thought and marijuana, meditating on movement in time, rolling, running, and the foolishness of it all, circling with no finality or purpose. All the world's frenetic activity seemed like nothing when imagining the greater mystery of the earth and the essence of things.

But I wasn't just meditating all day. I continued to practice the virtues my mother had taught me regarding earning my way and working. I had several jobs in various restaurants. One of my jobs was at a famous restaurant and bar in downtown Roanoke, with traditional, old-world style hardwood floors and tables. There, I washed dishes and prepped food for over a year. It was a high-paced job. All the wait staff and bartenders were in their 20s and early 30s. I worked the night shift, meeting the dinner rush. It was a popular place, especially on weekends. The pace was frenetic as the entire team tried to get all the food out on time without incident. Strangely, the fast pace was enjoyable; there was a rhythm to the madness, and I would feel a particular flow to it all, even in the chaos. Soon, I would come to find out, that most of the staff, as well as the owner, was using cocaine, which was partly the reason for the frenetic activity. I wasn't invited; I was too young for them and, as a dishwasher, too unimportant.

Nearly all the wait staff were beautiful women, but the bartender was a young man named Charley. He was interesting, not a typical burnout like my friends or my brother Russell. He was more gentlemanly, well-dressed, and worldly. He was adventurous like I thought myself to be. He had a BMW motorcycle, which was a draw for the young women working there. Often, during the heat of the frenetic restaurant activity, he and one of the young ladies would passionately kiss in the middle of the high-velocity rush, just for the sake of it. I looked up to him—envied him.

I already had a two-wheeled motorbike, and I loved it. Mine was a classic, Italian-made, blue Piaggio moped, but much smaller than his large motorcycle. Yet I could relate to his love of his bike. Riding my Piaggio was not fast and sleek (it even had dorky peddles), but the feeling of driving it in the open air was pure liberty.

Charley was a colorful man. In Roanoke, European bikes were rare; instead, Harley Davidson's were the norm. But he wasn't a southern Dixie redneck. He was cultured and began to tell me about Europe. He had just gotten back from there, having toured the continent alone on his BMW. I would anxiously listen to him whenever I could get his attention. He told me, "I shipped my BMW both to and from Europe. I spent my time touring around for several months throughout Germany, France, Spain, and Italy." He was getting ready to go back the following summer and was saving his bartender tips to do so. He would tell me, "I sleep for free, camping on my mat in the empty castles over there." He excited my dreams. I wanted to make a trip like this, too, and to be like him. That dream premonition I had as a twelve-year-old on Walnut Avenue to *see the world* just got bigger.

At this same time, my mother brought Europe directly into our home. She enrolled to be a host family for foreign exchange students, and we soon received a young intern from Spain named Blythe, who planned to live with us the entire nine-month school year. She and I were both sixteen-years-old when she came. She was a beautiful, confident girl, looking and dressing much different than a typical southern Roanoke girl. She was artistic in the way she dressed in earth-toned, tight fitting, colorful dresses and jewelry, and compact, curly, sandy brown hair. Her look was akin to Jennifer Beals of Flashdance fame. I appreciated her sense of fashion and style.

She told me about Madrid and the lively Mediterranean island of Ibiza in Spain, where her father lived. I had never met a girl from outside the U.S. before. There was a dignity and excitement to our little friendship.

There was another girl that had come to Roanoke from Spain as part of the same cultural exchange program. Blythe had not known her in Spain, but the two were now best friends. She lived in another home nearby. Her name flowed like a poem to my ears, Lucía. She was one year older than I was.

Lucía was tall and thin, having long black curly hair with a cowlick in her front bangs, forcing her hair to stand up. Her eyes were large and dark. Her skin was dark reddish in tone, her fingers long and sinuous, and her legs and arms toned and beautiful. She stood erect and held her head high. Her walk was gracious and smooth. Her personality was that of a playful, but very energetic, puppy. Her voice was confident and forceful in her annunciation. She dressed like an Egyptian queen, though still casual. She appeared like the paintings and sculptures I had seen in my mother's art books. She was pure magnificence, and best of all she was friendly with me. She, Blythe, and I were a set; we were a trio of friends, the *Three Musketeers* we mused. I had never had friends of this quality before. Being friends with them was a source of pure pleasure in my young life.

I was attracted to Lucía, but more than just attraction, I admired her. I suppose it was because I had long hair, was using drugs, had no culture or refinement, and had no interest in school; whereas she was a well-adjusted girl, getting good grades in school, not using drugs, and from a well to do family in Spain. She and I would often go out together. I would dress in my best artistically styled clothes for her. I would pick her up at her house, and she would ride on the back of my moped. The memory of her sitting behind me—with her arms wrapped around my waist as we drove 30 miles per hour on the shoulder of the road, with her high-sense of fashion, and long curly hair blowing in the wind—is one of the finest of my entire life. She was with me, a grubby drug user, a broken-home run away. I will never forget these moments.

But they were only moments. My life began to spiral downward even more. I quit the tenth grade after just one month. I had already been held back a year because the rehab Straight prevented me from attending school for six months, and I now found it hopeless to continue. Why should I care? Only my brother Francis had finished high school; the other three before me had all quit. All of my friends were doing drugs, smoking marijuana, and drinking.

I did have some thoughts of changing and improving my life. If anyone could have inspired me to change, it was Lucía. But I just wasn't ready to change, and she didn't want to embrace me for anything other than friendship. For me, though, this was sufficient: I would be whatever she allowed me to be. Of course, I tried and dreamt of more with her, but when rebuffed, I had too much admiration to do anything but respectfully accept her will. My mother taught me early in life that I must respect a woman if she is not ready. I did so. I felt lucky just to be able to call her my friend.

I did want more out of life, but I had gone so far down, and it felt too late to turn around. I don't know if what I felt for Lucía was love, but it was the most admiration mixed with attraction I have ever felt for anyone. I realized she was out of my league, and I weakly accepted that, accepting my own low self-esteem at the time.

She would graduate from high school that year and leave back for Spain. But I would yet get another chance to see her years later.

17. Family Handcuffs

When I was seventeen, I bought a 1974 compact Mercury Capri with a V6 and manual shifter—a speedy car. I had gotten my driver's license and was in the process of fixing it up. Before obtaining the license and plates, I took it out for a test drive. It could *get a wheel* not only in first gear but second as well. As I was burning rubber, a police officer who was half a mile away heard the tires screeching. He quickly found me and pulled me over right behind my home. I got out of the car to talk to him—my mind racing as to whether to run or stand. He was asking questions, and I got scared. I didn't want to be arrested, as I knew this might eventually mean me going back to Straight. So, I ran. I did what I had learned to do so many times before: run and run fast. I quickly lost the officer by foot.

But the officer knew who I was and spoke with my mother. Eventually, I had no other option than to turn myself in. When I did so, I was put into juvenile court proceedings and was eventually put into juvenile detention for several days.

My mother didn't like that I had dropped out of school, but as long as I was working and staying out of legal trouble, she would not fuss. But getting arrested and put into juvenile detention was too much. She habitually held in her feelings for long periods but would eventually have a breaking point. This was it. She was finished with me again. However, this time, instead of communicating it to me directly, she secretly plotted with my father.

Right after my release, I had a drug-fueled celebration with friends, and the next day was sleeping it off on the couch at home alone. Suddenly, my father appeared in my entire field of vision, shaking me and yelling, "Get up!" He had never stepped foot in my mother's home before, yet here he was, shaking me awake. He had driven from his home (having recently moved from Detroit to Cincinnati) to confront me, again. This time, he had a large muscular man with him who acted as an enforcer and guard. The two held me down and put me in handcuffs. My father yelled, "You are going back to Straight to complete the program!"

Being seventeen I was still a minor. I believed he had the legal right to put me back in Straight. This time my mother was no longer a hindrance, but fully consented to me going back. My father and his enforcer loaded me into the car's back seat in handcuffs and drove me from Virginia to Ohio, an eight-hour drive.

When we arrived at Straight on Sunday, the staff could not immediately accept me, so we had to wait for several hours. My father now lived just twenty minutes away from the facility in the town of Milford. Late that afternoon I sat with my father in his home—the guard ever present. Through some manipulation, I convinced my father to place the handcuffs in front, rather than behind my back so that I could eat something. I told him, "I promise, I'm ready to go back to Straight," even shedding real tears. I couldn't rebel as this would make things worse, and I did have regrets (as I was still coming down from drugs).

But my deeply rooted freedom instinct was taking over to control the situation as my mind also scoured a means of escape. As soon as he rearranged the handcuffs, I saw my opening. The only thing between Straight and my freedom was his front door. I rose and bolted as fast as I could, quickly unlocking the door from the inside. If I were unable to open it instantly, I would be captured as both of them were already coming after me. It was a risk, but I had nothing to lose.

It worked! I slid the lock over and dashed outside, running as fast as my legs could take me, even as I lacked balance without the ability to sway my arms—still shackled in cuffs. I ran fast, stumbling over myself as I flew across the neighbors' lawns. I had never been in this neighborhood before, but I just kept running, and soon, neither the guard nor my father could keep up. I kept running for fifteen minutes; it felt as if my heart was lodged in my throat trying to come out of my mouth. I ran through a gully and into a large, undeveloped tract of land near a hundred-foot water tower. I was a mile from my father's house and needed to rest. I kept out of sight, lying low to the ground below the grass and ridgeline. But it was getting late, and it was early winter. I had no jacket, wallet, or anything. Only the clothes on my back.

There was a gas station nearby that had an attached service garage. I staked it out for several minutes. A young man was attending the station alone. He looked like someone who likely smoked marijuana and partied, like myself and my friends. I needed help badly, so I decided to try to get it from him. I put my right hand in my right pocket and the left-hand sort of attached to my right belt loop. I did the best I could to hide the handcuffs. I approached him at dusk when no cars were present.

When he greeted me, he immediately noticed my strange predicament, a shining chain and cuff on my wrist. It was impossible to hide. I told him I had escaped from my father's house, who was trying to put me into Straight. He had heard about Straight, as many youths in the area had, and he decided to help me, believing it was a horrible brainwashing cult. He brought me into the attached garage to hide me until his friend came with bolt cutters. I would duck whenever a customer came for gas. About an hour later his friend came and cut off the handcuffs, a difficult task, but only slightly pinching my skin.

I couldn't believe what I had just endured, handcuffed by my own father, dragged across multiple state lines, and yet I escaped it all again. I was that deer of my dreams: I would not be tamed or lose my freedom without using my keen instincts for escape. I felt like a real escape artist and wild animal. It was my own *Escape from Warsaw*, that fascinating read of so many years prior.

It was night, and the station was closing. The attendant invited me to his house for the evening. We got in his car and headed there. He told his mother I was a friend of his, and she agreed I could stay the night. The next morning we had breakfast. He then gave me some winter clothing and dropped me off at the Florence Mall near Highway 75. It was the same mall I had stopped at many years earlier while hitchhiking to Florida. I was here again and now had to hitchhike.

Always on the watch for the possibility of my father looking for me, I started to hitchhike on the 75 south. I wasn't having any luck getting a ride. Suddenly snow started falling fast, and the on-ramp became a colossal wet mess. Sleet, snow, and ice drenched the area in just a few hours. I was sopping wet and bone cold. I took refuge in the mall and called my brother Russell in Roanoke, who agreed to come get me, but he couldn't get there until the next morning.

I had no money and was now a refugee. Both my parents wanted to have me arrested as a runaway and thrown into Straight. So that night I slept under a freeway bridge. It was freezing cold but relatively dry, in comparison to the snow drifts on the ground around it. The cement floor where I lay had rocks scattered all over. I would have to make due because I had no place else to sleep. The sound under the bridge was immense: the trucks harrowing through, creating a vortex of decibels and wind. I barely slept, waking up in extreme pain from one of my calf muscles contracting. Because of the intense pain, I feared I would roll down the fifty-foot bridge embankment. After a minute, the painful contraction subsided, and by then morning came.

This was a moment I would never forget, nor would I wish on anyone. There was physical pain, but the emotional angst was far worse. The humiliation of it. I had recently been with two beautiful European girls in a home full of art, and now I was freezing cold, trying to sleep on a cement bed of rocks under a busy freeway bridge during a snowstorm—parentless and homeless. I let out a blood-curdling existential scream of pain . . . but also of freedom.

The next morning I met my brother. He bought me a cup of hot coffee and a big hearty breakfast at a local diner (a meal I remember to this day). We drove back to Roanoke through the snowstorm, which had gotten much worse. On the car ride home, I felt a strange detachment from the idea of family. I was sure I didn't want to go back to Straight. But I didn't know what I would do now. Both parents were united in putting me back inside. I had to wait it out somewhere. I had to stay hidden for several months until reaching the age of majority.

18. The End of Straight

That was the last I would see of Straight; I was to turn eighteen in a few months and would be free of it forever. For many years following, my father believed Straight helped me. He thought that since I never complained to him while I was inside, that I must have liked it there. The truth is, we were not allowed to criticize, or we would be punished in rap sessions or pushed back a phase. This was Straight's way of hiding the truth from parents, and the reason so many parents went along with it. The hard marketing sell of staff was a key to the program: *If you don't trust us with your kid, he or she will die on the streets, go to prison, or be put into a psychiatric ward.* Those were the choices.

Yet I was not necessarily on this path, and, in fact, many other members of Straight were not as well. My heart was not about high crimes and deadly drugs. I had a heart for freedom and experiencing the outdoors, not confinement and force. Straight never inspired me to change.

By 1993 Straight was forced to shut down, following state regulatory complaints, allegations of Medicare fraud, and several lawsuits that resulted in millions of dollars. These claims included rape, false imprisonment, excessive restraint, deprivation of food and water, and the denial of the right to attend school.[10] All of this took part in a for-profit endeavor that encouraged lengthy stays to perpetuate financial benefit. In fact, many of the most extended members were those who had doctors or lawyers as parents, who could afford to pay year after year.

Until recently I had repressed my memories of Straight. I was forced to research it to write about my experiences there, and this research opened up floodgates of sadness and anger. I recently went to visit the old facility, which now houses a Muslim Community Center, whose staff graciously allowed me (and two other former members) to enter and look around. I went in the hope I could remember more. I, along with many others, have suffered what is called in psychological terms *disassociation*: the suppression of memories that are too painful to recall.

One of the two former members with whom I toured the facility had remembered me (having recalled my first escape and forcible return). He was tearful during our visit and told us of having been raped by his oldcomer when he first entered the program. He would continue the program for several years, eventually becoming a staff member, until he finally had a change of heart, then testifying against Straight in several lawsuits, which forced Straight to pay large sums of money and eventually shut down.

Some of my research has revealed shocking truths. For example, many members had not even used drugs but were kept inside anyway as *dry druggies*, someone who would *potentially use* because of their attitude. I have heard stories of girls having been forced (or highly encouraged) to have abortions while in the program so as not to interfere with their progress. I have heard firsthand accounts of people over the age of eighteen who were kidnapped and held by Straight. It is no surprise then that there are a disproportionate number of ex-members who have killed themselves following this program.[11]

It has only just dawned on me that Straight may have held me in contravention of the law. I thought I was legally required to remain in this program, yet my parents never obtained any court order to place me there. How does a minor child legally argue that he is not required to remain when his parents and officials all say he is? Back in the 1980s there was not such a spirit of individual rights as there is today, and the statute of limitations has long since expired to file a lawsuit against Straight for falsely imprisoning me; but if I could, I would.

Mel Sembler, the founder of Straight, later went on to be appointed an ambassador to Australia and then to Italy for all the political fundraising he had done for the Republican Party. I have recently seen Freedom of Information (FOIA) documents that show Straight and the White House had direct, friendly communications, particularly during the litigation of civil lawsuits that shut Straight down.

Now, Mel and his wife Betty Sembler are the founders of the Drug Free America Foundation. On their website, they prominently state that they have successfully treated 12,000 youths through Straight.[12] In truth, 50,000 youth went through its doors. Can it be success that only 20 percent were treated successfully? And of these 20 percent, how many have lasting sobriety without psychological problems? And what of the other 80 percent? Their method of attack therapy perpetrated by children has had lasting effects on thousands of former members. Denying a child freedom, outdoors, and education while screaming at them for over twelve hours a day for months cannot end well.

Straight was like the re-education camps one hears of in former communist nations like Vietnam. The idea was to completely clear the brain of old history and habits by applying a steamroller to it. But the heart yearns for freedom and will always find it, rebelling against force. Parents cannot love their child so much as to prevent their freedom. This kind of love will lead to hatred by the child. How does a child learn to trust others after this?

Today, I can recognize that the mind is a delicate instrument and that perhaps some of the lessons I learned in Straight improved my life, like the realization that my drug use was entirely selfish and hurtful to others and myself. But there are too many negative lessons I learned, like fear and distrust of others in authority and in family relationships.

In my life since Straight, trust has been hard for me. When relationships get difficult, my first instinct is to run. Straight helped me to define myself as a person that runs and never stops. You could say this is a permanent scar on my soul. Yet I do not see myself as a victim. Instead, I am proud of all my earlier running and escapes. It led to nightmares for many years, but these nightmares were exciting for me. I wouldn't change this, but I know I should improve in trusting others.

But then I did have a problem: I was using marijuana and LSD, skipping school, running away, and committing misdemeanors and traffic crimes. My father and mother faced a dilemma in dealing with me. What to do? Neither of them had grown up seeing such drug use in the home. The '70s and '80s saw an explosion of youth experimenting with drugs. There was no book on how to deal with the matter. I understand the perspective of my parents.

My father put me in Straight out of fear that I would get much worse. He did what he thought was best, given the options of the time, within the framework of what he knew. Like many of his day, he bought into the marketing and public relations generated by Straight. While I do not believe in judging the past by today's standards, with the benefit of hindsight, I believe sending me to a disciplined boarding school or a summer abroad program may have been more helpful than locking me inside a windowless cement facility, where I was branded a druggie and forced to participate in attack therapy.

Much later in life, I would learn a valuable lesson: to keep my mind and soul truly free and at peace, I must remain one hundred percent sober. This was not something that I understood in my youth or that was taught to me in

Straight. It was not something all the force in the world could show. It would only come from the experience of life itself and by accepting the will of God.

19. The Traveling Circus

Shortly after I arrived back in Roanoke, while staying with my brother, I went to see the circus as it passed through town. While there I noticed a *Job Wanted* posting. The job was a traveling one, going to different cities throughout the country. I had no other ideas of how I could stay out of the sight of my parents for the rest of the year until turning eighteen when I would gain my legal freedom. My mother and father would not know where I was, being in a different city every few days. Besides, it seemed a romantic way to see the country.

I was hired as a laborer, putting up and taking down the big tents. The pay was minimum wage, but the most important part for me was that they provided free food from the vendors and bunk beds in the circus trucks for sleeping. The circus was set to leave Roanoke the following night for a city in Tennessee.

The next evening I reported for work. In the dark of night, I climbed into the back of a cargo truck that was fitted out with several bunk beds, enough for about ten laborers. The driver then shut the cargo door on those of us inside, saying, "Y'all aren't going to be able to get out of this truck until morning when we get to the circus site in Tennessee. If you have to piss, do so out of this little crack near the door. See you tomorrow." And with that, he shut and locked the cargo door.

I slept on one of the lower bunks. The man above me was drinking straight out of a liquor bottle. As he drank himself to sleep, he urinated in his cot, and it dripped down onto mine. When it came time for me to urinate, I did so the proper way (as I was instructed), getting most of it to go outside onto the moving road. I slept just one hour that night, rolling around amidst loud snoring and choking from the smell of stale urine and alcohol.

When the door was opened from the outside early the next morning, the sun's light came flooding in, revealing my first good look at my new colleagues: dirty men without teeth, shower-less, muscular, all with hardened faces and dark eyes. My romantic vision of joining the traveling circus was imploding.

I went to work for the next ten hours, using thirty-pound mallets to hammer large spikes into the ground that held up the massive canvas tents.

My extremely muscular colleagues were not phased, but my body was worn out by the end, not yet used to this intense toil.

After a very long day raising the tents, I got the afternoon and following day off while the circus shows entertained the public. During this time I walked behind the tents in the employee and animal corral areas. There I saw the trainers beating the elephants and horses. They thrashed them with sharp-edged whips, screaming profanities at them. During the show the trainers would act friendly, smiling, and treating the animal respectfully; but after the show, if the animal had made any mistake, they would be beaten with the trainers' entire physical force. These were miserable men, living in a world of anger. It was so brutal—they would draw blood from the animals. It made me sick.

Pulling my eyes away, I continued walking past the trailers where the entertainers lived. There were all kinds of strange people: contorted acrobats, dwarf men, deformed women, and sad clowns. I could see and hear sexual activity all around. There was a sick feeling in the air. I wanted nothing to do with such a bizarre and mean life. I quit while still in Tennessee. They paid me my wages, and I hitched my way back to Roanoke.

20. The Age of Majority

The next few months I continued to live with my brother and friends, often crashing on various couches. I was working an erratic night job at a fruit and produce transport company. I would be paid fifty dollars to unload each tractor-trailer that came in, full of banana boxes. The boxes were fifty pounds each, and it would take several hours to unload each trailer (at a rapid pace). It was a fast way to make money. One night while working, a colleague had a needle kit, and asked, "Do you want to shoot-up some cocaine?" I had tried everything else by then, even crack, so I tried it. It did little for me though; perhaps the cocaine was not strong enough. But I decided never to try it again. I didn't like the idea of it, damaging my veins for a high. I wanted to stay with the natural herb of marijuana and the occasional use of LSD. I had always been a peace-loving, calm person, who was against violence, and now a lover of nature. I didn't like uppers or speed of any kind. Perhaps I was lucky that the cocaine was no good. Had the surge of shooting up been as euphoric as many claim it to be, maybe I would have gotten addicted as so many do.

My brother Russell had recently moved to Franklin County about twenty miles from Roanoke. Franklin is considered the Deep South and is known as the moonshine capital of the world because it produces so much of the illegal whiskey, even today. But he came to Roanoke often. He and I had a friend who lived at the base of Mill Mountain. This house, where I usually slept, became a full-time *party house*, where there were keg and drug parties nearly every night. At one of those parties, someone had a homemade tattoo machine, a needle with Indian ink attached to a little model-car electric motor with a small battery. Having a gentle nature, I decided to get a peace sign on my upper right-back shoulder blade. It was a '60s throwback symbol since I loved all the '60s music and the idea of peace and love. After a while, I thought it looked bland, like a prison-style tattoo, so I eventually paid a professional to fill it in with a colorful sunburst. Much later in life, I was to have several laser treatments to remove it, though I have a shadow of it left, to remind me of my past.

My eighteenth birthday finally came. Now I was free from Straight forever, no longer having to watch my back for potential kidnapping by my father or anyone else. I celebrated with my brother and several friends as we drunk what is called gooseberry moonshine. Gooseberry is a wild berry, giving the 190 proof drink a fruity taste. The fruit infuses the alcohol and vice versa. After a couple of swigs, I blacked out.

This was how I saw my freedom then. Everything was a cause for the celebration of drunkenness and drugs.

Later that year my mother started to allow me to come and visit, to eat at her home and to see her, and sometimes stay over if I needed. Russell had recently bought a beautiful blue and white two-toned Oldsmobile Cutlass with white leather seats. After a night of heavy drinking, we planned to sleep at our mother's place, so we drove there. At about 2 a.m. and nearly a mile from my mother's home, we rammed into a large tree. The car's front end broke the tree in half—the lower half nearly uprooted entirely from the earth, and the upper half was lying on top of the car. The entire front end was smashed in with the grill standing erect about two feet high. Miraculously the car was still running. We both mused that being so drunk probably saved our lives since if our bodies were tense (folklore my brother taught me), we could have gone through the windshield. Bruised and battered, we took off for home, hoping no cop would see us in the five minutes left to drive.

My mother's house had a large privacy fence around the back where the driveway was. There was an indentation in the fence so that we could park our car outside the gate in our driveway, or we could open the gate and pull the car inside. The indentation had a *No Parking* sign since it shared a parking lot with a local bar whose patrons would block our fence opening. We planned to pull in, open the fence, and drive in so the car would be hidden. But to our great dismay, a police officer was sitting in the indentation of our fence, waiting to bust drunk patrons that were exiting the bar. He was not allowed to park there, as it was my mother's property, but there he was. We did not see him until we pulled near the entry because the fence indentation hid his car. It was too late to stop and turn around. We were pulling in and had to reorient and try to continue across the lot immediately. Our hearts started to race. We hoped beyond hope that he did not see us drive right in front of him. But, of course, it is impossible to be inconspicuous with a smashed car, moaning and smoking in the night. He pulled behind us as we were trying to drive up the hill to the front of the house. The car stalled mid-way. The officer arrested my brother for drunk driving. Russell went to jail for DUI, but I was allowed to go home. But my mother never found out since he was an adult and no longer lived with her.

New Year's Eve arrived, and my brother Russell and I went out partying as we did on so many occasions. He didn't have a car anymore, but we prowled around on foot. We had drunk so much that I was in a state of semi-consciousness. We wanted more beer, so he attempted to distract a convenience store clerk while I tried to put a six pack of beer in my jacket and run out of the store. Because we were so drunk, the clerk easily detained us until the police arrived. But just as they were reaching us, Russell and I ran. He ran up a hill and tripped, rolling back down the hill into the arms of the police. I ran fast but was tackled by officers. We were both thrown into a paddy wagon and spent the night in the local jail. I was charged with *concealed goods*. I pled guilty and got my first—and only—adult conviction. After court, I was to spend ten days in jail, but they released me after just four hours. My mother never found out as I was an adult now.

The conviction seemed insignificant at the time, but to this day it's still on my record. Every time I've applied for a job since then I've had to list this crime. It's like my tattoo, a permanent remembrance of my youth.

21. Rambling to California

Nothing worked for me in Roanoke anymore. All that existed for me was drugs, alcohol, arrests, and now a criminal conviction. After serving time, I was finished with the requirements of my conviction. That feeling that had never gone away, to *see the world*, was calling louder now. I had to get out of Roanoke. I had only been on the east coast of the U.S., and I wanted to go west and see California. An acquaintance named Greg, older than me by about ten years, had a car and wanted an adventure too. He had a live-in girlfriend and a baby, but leaving them didn't seem to bother him. We decided to go to California together in his blue, four-door Chevy Nova. The only requirement I had was that he not shoot-up or deal in hard drugs. I had heard some rumblings about his past involvement with heroin, and I didn't want that trouble around me. "I overcame my habit," he assured me.

Greg was shady, but I needed a traveling partner. He was a southern purebred, uneducated, a small-time drug dealer with a pockmarked face, southern-style clothing and drawl, Dixie belt buckle, long bell-bottom style pants, and a chain wallet. He was not a handsome guy or charismatic but was an excellent scammer I would find out.

He said his goodbyes to his family, and I said my goodbyes to my friends and mother. We took off to Florida first. Not having much money, we slept in the Nova. It was broad enough to sleep horizontally curled up on the seats—Greg in the front and me in the rear.

When we got to Florida, we started to head west out of the panhandle. There, we picked up a hitchhiker named Angel, who had a small dog with him named Kimba. Angel was an odd man, introverted with thick-rimmed glasses. He was a marijuana grower. He tended to his plants in Florida during winter months and other plants in Oregon in the summer months. Since winter was ending, he was heading back to Oregon. He rode with us and taught us some tips on how to camp along the highways. He had a multi-function pocketknife attached to his belt. He always had this with him and told us, "This little knife never leaves me; it's always tied to me right here."

The three of us stopped in New Orleans. We walked down Bourbon Street in the French Quarter and drank Hurricanes, the favorite strong drink. There were plenty of half-drunk glasses on the street, so we drank those since we were short on money to buy our own. As we were walking along the busy pedestrian thoroughfare, Angel's dog Kimba spotted a woman in a wheelchair, got excited, and ran toward the woman, jumping onto her lap. She went into a frenzy: "Get that damn dog off of me, fools!" The police came on the scene to calm the commotion and told us to leave since dogs were not allowed on Bourbon Street. We met a local who had a crash pad, and we all went there to sleep on the floor.

The next morning we continued on our way west toward Texas, but it was slow going since we had a minimal amount of money for fuel. We often stole it by siphoning it, or we asked people for gas money at rest stops. Greg showed me how to do this. We had a story that our car needed repairs, and we were on our way home to Virginia. Once a man told us that he knew we were scammers because our Virginia plated car was on the westbound rest stop (not in the easterly direction of home), but gave us a few dollars for having a creative story.

Since our progress west was slow, Angel, anxious to get to a friend's house in Southern California, ended up leaving us by hitchhiking on. But he wanted to meet us later in California, so he gave us an address where to find him when we arrived there. He wanted to go north with us after our rendezvous.

Just the two of us again, Greg and I took a side trip to Big Bend National Park in Texas, then known as the deadliest park in the world. It is a desert, full of sharp plants, sharp rocks, insects that bite, cobras, and other wild and dangerous animals.

The first day we paid a small canoe paddler a couple of dollars to bring us to the Mexico side of the Rio Grande. We walked around in Mexico but were told to be careful, not to wander far because of dangerous drug traffickers. There was supposedly a small town nearby that was so dangerous that if we went, we would find trouble. Perhaps it was a myth since we saw no such town. Eventually, we made our way back to the U.S. side in the same canoe. Several Mexicans were selling food in makeshift concessions on both sides of the river. We enjoyed a small snack as we watched many Mexicans coming across to the U.S. side. The crossing was utterly unregulated.

Later that day we went for a walk in the desert, of course lighting up our marijuana pipe. My meditative mind began to enjoy the spiritualness of the rocks and desert . . . until we got lost and could not find our way back to the car. After a few hours we had run out of water, and we grew agitated and nervous. Marijuana had a spiritual side effect on me but also dumbed my perception, impeding my keen sense of judgment and direction. As I climbed a hill trying to find a way out, a sharp cactus plant drove into my leg about an inch. Blood was dripping all over my leg and shoe. After several hours, seeing the same rocks over and over, seemingly going in circles, we eventually found our way back to the car. It could have been much worse; one could die in that desert very quickly without water, food, or shelter.

That night we slept in a canyon on the banks of the Rio Grande. The wind whipped up so heavy that sand entered my exposed sleeping bag. I didn't get much sleep that night as the sand in my bag swirled in a vortex, and the wind outside was howling like a living ghost. But it was refreshing to crawl out of the bag in the listless morning with the sun peeking around the canyon walls. All the dirt under my fingernails was gone; I felt as if I had been cleansed by sandblasting.

We headed out of the park to El Paso, where we parked our car to cross the border into Juarez, Mexico. We walked over the bridge and into Benito Juarez, the main thoroughfare. We didn't go into any of the drinking clubs for lack of money, but their doors were wide open as hucksters tried to get us inside. Everywhere around these clubs were prostitutes and dark, wiry men wandering about—lost in sexual desire.

One of the open-door clubs had a sign that said *Donkey Show* in English. Curious about what that was, I peeked around the door into the club. I will never forget what I saw there. The image is burned into my mind even today: an aroused donkey was tied up by all fours, hanging from the ceiling upside down, with a naked woman attempting to mount him sexually. I felt sick looking at it. It repulsed me. I didn't dare to look longer. It was so unnatural. My feet would not cross the door threshold; my body had frozen. It was to be my first taste of the sickness of unadulterated lust. Evil was present. It was as if a wild and ferocious beast was free, bucking in the streets, destroying the very souls of men and women. I had seen pornography before in Playboy magazines, but this was not the glorification of the female body. This was brutality.

Much later in life, I learned of an immaterial entity named Asmodeus, a demon of lust, responsible for twisting the sexual desires of men. Even though I did not know the existence of this devil, it was he I saw there that day.

Before leaving Juarez, we bought two bottles of Mezcal tequila that had the mescaline worm inside. This worm eats the inside of a cactus that has psychedelic properties, and when a human eats the worm he is supposed to hallucinate, not unlike LSD. But we learned that the worm was no longer psychedelic. Rather than a worm eating the plant, now corporations grow and harvest the worms on an organized farm to produce them in volume. These lack the psychedelic properties. We were disappointed as we heard the folklore of this native and natural style psychedelic trip and wanted to try it.

We took the two bottles and walked back across into the U.S., but not without being stopped by border agents. I had left my identification in the car, but the agents allowed me back in after some questioning.

This was my first taste of international travel. I had up to that point only traveled with my parents to a few U.S. states and Windsor, Canada (which felt the same as the U.S.). I was now seeing an entirely new world, a seedy and dark world, but a new one nonetheless. It was exhilarating to be able to live free and effectuate my childhood dreams to *see the world*.

We headed west into New Mexico and stopped for the night at high elevation. We drank much of the tequila and passed out. The next morning we awoke to the soft flutter of snow on the roof of the car; we had slept through a snowstorm. Nearly two feet of snow had fallen that night; the car was covered. It was considered a freak storm since it was spring. But within two hours of the hot desert sun rising, all the snow nearly melted in a slush pile, and we continued our way westward.

We finally reached California and crossed the border at a little town whose name reminded me of my friend from Spain: the village of Blythe. When we arrived in southern California, we picked up Angel at the rendezvous address. The three of us did some exploring around Los Angeles. We went to Hollywood to walk the Star Walk. Back then, it was a high drug use area, and we were regularly propositioned to buy drugs. Greg and I decided to try PCP for the first time, smoking a cigarette dipped in it for just five dollars. As a result, we ended up fearfully cowering in a local park (I believe it was Echo Park), unable to function. I thought I had lost my senses. Angel didn't use any drugs except marijuana, so he helped us to fare. I was never to try PCP again; it created feelings of fear and anger in me—emotions that did not suit my more sensitive nature.

22. Santa Cruz Hippies

After recovering our senses, the three of us headed north, eventually winding up in Santa Cruz. As we walked around downtown, we met some marijuana smoking Native Americans, who invited us to stay in a clandestine hippie camp in the Henry Cowell Redwoods State Park—just north of the city on Highway 9. The park is an enormously dense and lush green forest without any development for miles around. Some of the trees are immense, old-growth redwoods. The San Lorenzo, a fast-flowing river in parts, and a trickle in other parts, winds its way through the park.

The camp sounded intriguing, so we let the Native Americans lead us there. Most, if not all, of the hippies in the camp lacked cars. But the forest and camp were within walking distance (about five miles) of the city. A vehicle could reach a parking lot on Highway 9 about a mile from the camp, but the actual camp itself could only be reached by foot.

We had a car but wanted to know the walk route from town. The hike followed railroad tracks, eventually over a trestle and into the forest, until the intersection of a secret trail. The hidden trail led in about a mile until arrival at the clandestine camp. It was utterly primitive: there was no structures, no toilets, and no running water. The only way to bring in water was to lug large water containers up the mountain from the San Lorenzo River.

We ended up staying for several weeks. There were on average twenty to thirty other campers there—many of them Native Americans. I had my own tent as many also had but not all. Some had fabric or plastic lean-tos, and some just risked the rain and slept on a mat near the firepit, under the stars—that is, when one could sleep. Most nights were party nights; everyone would trip on LSD, smoke marijuana, take magic mushrooms, and drink alcohol. We spent our time like nature nymphs, moving around a campfire circle, playing drums and other wooden instruments. It was a pagan festival, fueled by drugs, with the pipes of pan continually calling.

Many of the Native Americans had assumed self-styled leadership roles. Their authority came from their declaration that they were indigenous to the land, and the rest of us were European invaders. They would tell us stories about their traditions and of the Great Spirit and Mother Earth. They had a mystical way of telling stories under the great fires we made in the dead of night. The flames leaped over fifty feet into the air under a brightly lit dome of stars.

While high on drugs, the Native Americans kept their balance and composure much better than the European white men at the camp. But this applied only if they did not drink alcohol. Their tolerance for alcohol was much lower than the rest, impeding their keen perception. For us white Europeans, deadening our perception was the purpose of drinking. But these Native Americans, by nature, did not react well to this deadening feeling: they acted like an injured animal in a fight for its life. Instead of getting mild and sloppy as most, the Natives became angry and mean. They would scare us, mostly by their wild eyes and crazy impassioned stories of the dangers lurking in the woods. It felt as if violence was just a step away.

The whites in the camp had an ideological admiration for the Native Americans. We all began to accept that they were the rightful owners of the land we were standing on. The invader enemy was the Christian missionaries that took over their land 500 years earlier. The Natives in our camp considered themselves shamans and rejected the over-industrialized world of work and development. This was my first taste of this new alternative way of thinking about the world.

I liked these anti-industrialist ideas; they fit my love for nature I had discovered in Roanoke's Evergreen Cemetery. But I was never a blind follower of ideas or people, no matter how charismatic they appeared to be. To me, these Native American shamans were irrationally cultish and hucksters. I did not entirely buy into the idea that they had a special relationship to Mother Earth or had a stronger right to the land. Part of my doubt was because they didn't work. In fact, the entire camp didn't work. The purpose of the camp was to do drugs and live outside of social norms for basically no cost. Being raised on the virtue of work and industriousness, I couldn't accept their assumed authority.

Everything was as free as possible since no one had money. For food, we would all go to the St. Francis Soup Kitchen. This was a way of life for the hippies, but something I had never done before. It was located right off the train tracks, so it was easy to get to. I had respect for this soup kitchen and felt the dignity of the place.

There was a church high on a hill above the soup kitchen amidst forested pines. It had a spiritual beauty to it. Soup kitchen volunteers from the church were helping feed grown and able men who didn't care about work and wouldn't take care of themselves.

I have since revisited this soup kitchen, which is still in existence, and I learned the name of the church, which remains high on the hill above. It is the Holy Cross Catholic Church. Today, the hippies are still there, and while the nature ideology still exists, there are far more lost souls strung out on drugs— most having lost everything because of crack. Several of the homeless have bicycles with small trailers, which they bring back and forth from the soup kitchen into the woods where they live. The geography has not changed. The train tracks are still the route the homeless take back and forth into the woods. Today there is much violence as well. One of the current volunteers told me a recent story of some homeless who scalped another while wasted on drugs. It seems the peace and love LSD hippies had long since become outnumbered.

Back then we had two other methods to get food besides the soup kitchen. One was dumpster diving. In Santa Cruz, restaurants and grocery stores would throw out perfectly good food. We would collect fresh and voluminous food from these dumpsters (mostly the food having reached its expiration date), sometimes even alcohol (as when a case of beer would have one bottle broken, the store would throw the entire case out). We would make a special drive to score at one of the most fecund of dumpsters in the region, at a place called Half Moon Bay. What a wonderful name for a place, I thought; there was genuine mysticism breathing in the air among the pines, the fog, and sea of Half Moon Bay.

Our group also had a scam to get large food boxes to bring back to the camp. It was a social service program that each person had to apply for. If granted, one could get one box a week. Many of the hippies could no longer get a box because they were banned for abusing the program. But I was able to get my box. I brought it to the camp, and it was devoured within an hour because so many people were sharing it.

The camp was communal, so all things were shared, not in an organized way but in a chaotic state of nature way, with peace and love adjectives tossed about to provide enough rationale and guilt. Instead of share and share alike, it felt more like there were mostly takers with just a few providers.

Greg and I took frequent trips to the Bay Area, specifically Berkeley. Berkeley was a wild, drug-fueled campus town; it felt as if the police didn't care what sort of illegal drug use occurred, as compared to Roanoke where police were always on the prowl. We would go to the Martin Luther King Jr. Park, where I started to buy sheets of LSD to resell at the camp for a profit. The first sheet paid for itself in sales, and the rest was all profit. The park was then, and still is today, full of homeless and drug users.

On the drive back to the camp on Highway 1, we would often stop at a nude beach on the Pacific Ocean (I believe it may have been Bonny Doon). We never went naked as this was not something a burnout or redneck would do. We only went to look at the handful of nude women. We were two long-haired, grungy druggies—Greg with his chain wallet and me with my boots and beard, ogling at the nude women. Sometimes naked men (who were far more in number) would walk by; but out of embarrassed masculinity, Greg and I would look away. The men would look at us in disgust as we flung our cigarette butts on the sand, uncomfortably laughing like a couple lustful, insecure boys.

I was the youngest in the camp, and I was now providing a good part of the food and LSD. I was growing tired of the immaturity in the camp, grown men doing nothing but tripping at night, sleeping all day, and trying to scam for food. For the past several years, even as a pre-teen, I worked in various jobs. My mother had taught me the value of work, and that lesson remained rooted in me.

Because of this virtue, after three weeks dawdling in the camp, I went out to find a job. I easily found one at a local futon factory, stuffing mattresses, right near the railroad tracks and soup kitchen. When the rest of the camp heard, they were all pleased, since to my consternation, they now believed I would help contribute cash to the camp as well.

Meanwhile, Greg began to spend time with other people from the camp, disappearing with his car for long stretches at a time. He had been gone for several days and had my bag of personal items in the trunk of his car. When he finally returned, I went to fetch my bag, and when I opened the trunk, I noticed a small bag of needles for shooting up drugs. I confronted him, and he admitted to me, "Yea man, I'm shooting up, so what?" I told him, "I don't want to travel with you anymore. I don't want the trouble of this and don't want problems with the cops." He didn't argue. He informed me that he would be leaving with his new friends to see the Grateful Dead in Los Angeles. I retrieved my items, and he left the camp. I have never seen or heard from him since. Our friendship had ended, and my transportation was gone.

That night I arrived back in the camp, and most of the people were tripping on LSD. Someone told me that Angel, who had never used any drugs before other than marijuana, decided to try LSD for the first time. I looked to his tent and could see his silhouette inside, behind a small flashlight. He was acting strange, reaching into the air at phantoms. This is not unusual for someone tripping but looked eerie to me now, primarily because it was his first time. It's not safe to be tripping on LSD alone, as he had isolated himself away from the group (he was a loner at heart). Getting lost in the woods was always a danger, especially in the dense forests there. Moreover, the Native Americans had scared everyone by telling stories about another hippie camp nearby that was supposedly full of violent men. Whether or not the story was true, their folklore infected our minds.

I went to bed that night in my tent, feeling that everything had come undone. Greg, who started to use hard drugs again, had left with the car that had brought me to California. I felt sad for his girlfriend and child in Roanoke as I knew he was heading for major trouble in intravenous drug use. Now I was in a hippie camp with men older than me who were acting irresponsibly and living on free food from generous social and religious programs, and these same men wanted to take my money earned from working to help buy things for the camp. I was completely ready to leave this childish communal playground. At least I had a job, and I imagined perhaps I could find an apartment as I had done in St. Petersburg years before. But the next morning would not only change my plans but change my sense of innocence forever.

23. A Missing Angel

That morning Angel was not in his tent, and no one could find him. The people who had stayed up that night said Angel left his tent in the middle of the night and didn't come back. Several of us went looking for him. We all feared that he got lost while on his first LSD trip or, worse, that the rival camp full of twisted men had taken him.

I looked all morning, yelling his name. Finally, I found his clothes on the bank of the San Lorenzo River, near the train tracks, less than a mile from the road. His pants and shirt were rolled up neatly, lying next to a fallen tree. But strangely, his underwear and shoes were also there, placed neatly together. My heart sank when I noticed his small pocketknife lying there, unattached from his pants. He never parted with this, as he told me when I met him in Florida. I had never seen him without it. Here it was, unattached to him, lying there with all of his clothes, yet he was nowhere in sight. Dread filled my mind.

I began to think perhaps he committed suicide by drowning in the river, or maybe he jumped in front of a train. But his body was nowhere. I thought maybe the evil men from the other camp took him by force, but his clothes were neatly rolled up (he was a neat person), so it was logical to think he walked off naked, voluntarily. Perhaps he had an awful LSD trip. I had grown up hearing stories of people that have had bad trips and never woken out of them; for example, this was the rumor about Syd Barrett of Pink Floyd. I had seen others have bad trips and experienced mild ones myself, though I never experienced someone disappearing naked.

My soul was blackened. I was upset that Angel tried LSD, and this was the result. I called the police right away from a local pay phone to report him missing in the woods. My best guess was that he stripped naked while on LSD and went off wandering on foot, eventually getting lost. I could only hope he found his way back or that someone rescued him. But I was done. I wanted out of that camp. I gathered my things and left.

I will never forget him. Today, I feel remorse for having been a bad example. I feel moral responsibility and shame. To this day I have no idea what came of him. I have since called the detective's office to see whatever may have come of him but never received a call back from them.

My conscience was awakening as I began to see this dark side of life. Music and lyrics of darkness were one thing, but the reality of darkness was much harder on my heart and soul. My life was on the wrong track. I didn't want to live in hippie camps, eating free food, using drugs, and mooching off others. But what would I do? How was I going to live my life?

I decided not to try to find an apartment in town but to leave and cross the country, hitchhiking back to Virginia. My conscience had not told me to quit drugs or convert my life, however. I was not ready for that. I still had a hit of LSD left, which I took before starting my hitchhiking journey. It disabled me for a few hours; I ended up sitting in a park surrounded by houses in Santa Cruz, despondent about what had happened and about the long road of hitchhiking ahead. As I sat there, I noticed a beautiful woman in red, working outside of her home. I felt inside me a desire for home and the love of a woman. I cried of remorse, of loss, and of longing while high on LSD.

Finally, I assembled myself and started hitchhiking. One of my first rides was not going due east but instead north to Washington State. I decided to go along since the driver had a camper truck with plenty of food. He lived and traveled in a delivery truck, creatively converted into a camper. In the back, he had his bed, food, cookery, clothes, water, and his Harley Davidson motorcycle.

The first evening we camped on an Indian reservation near Crater Lake, Oregon. But we left early in the morning out of fear of harassment by the Native Americans. My ride told me that these Natives don't like trespassers and would even kill violators. We continued to the Washington border. He was heading north, and I decided to head east. We parted.

I then got a ride that took me along the Columbia River Gorge, passing the hundreds of waterfalls peppering the side of the highway—all sparkling under the sun's bright, shimmering rays. This was the lushest of nature I had yet seen in my short life. I would later learn it was the western terminus of the famous Lewis and Clark expedition.

I was then offered a ride to Reno, Nevada, which was south, but at least it was not going further out of my way. By the time my ride dropped me in Reno, I had no money left. I stole five dollars of tip money off a table at a casino restaurant. I got something to eat and used a little of the tip money to play the slot machines. To my surprise and elation, I began winning until I had nearly fifty dollars. I kept playing, but my winning streak had soon ended, and I started to lose. I decided to stop playing when my winnings were down to twenty-five dollars and quit while ahead.

I started hitchhiking east again and met a man on a highway ramp also trying to hitch out of Reno. I had planned to begin hitching on the same ramp, but now, as per hitchhiker's etiquette (first come first serve), I would have to continue to the next ramp to try to get a ride. But I stopped to talk with him for a moment before moving on. He was an older gentleman, wearing a tieless suit and holding a briefcase. He looked completely out of place as a hitchhiker: business like but dejected and forlorn. He told me, "I lost everything, my car and life savings, playing in the casinos. All I can do is hitchhike home." How could he have been so stupid to gamble his car away, I thought.

But wasn't I the stupid one? I had graduated from a Florida hitchhiker to the big leagues of cross-country hitching, and I was already meeting tragedy. Ominous clouds circled in the desert sky; things were to get much worse ahead.

24. Despair in Nebraska

In a very short time, I made it from Reno to Salt Lake City and then on to the Wyoming/Nebraska border. My ride dropped me off at the very first exit in western Nebraska. It was between here and the third Nebraskan exit where I would spend the next several days in a state of bitter demoralization.

The first day I spent the entire day with my thumb up, unable to get a ride. I slept on the side of the highway that night. I had no money left, it was cold, and I was alone. The second day, I got a ride all of five miles to the next exit. The driver told me, "People are afraid to pick up hitchhikers around here since a few months back, a hitchhiker murdered a truck driver right on this highway." Everyone had heard about it, and no one wanted to pick up hitchhikers.

Again, I held up my thumb all day without another ride.

I had only my thoughts all day and night, thinking about what led me here: about Greg who returned to being a junkie, leaving me without transportation; about Angel who disappeared; about all those irresponsible selfish hippies in the forest; about my two beautiful friends from Spain; and about all the crap I had done with my life. I couldn't take it—two days of rejection, freeway noise, and loneliness. I was screaming at the top of my lungs to whoever was in the heavens listening: "Help me!" I was losing my mind, and my emotional state was crumbling, bleeding into the flat plains of Nebraska.

Another night came, and I had to sleep on the side of the highway again. In two full days, I had gone five miles.

The third day more of the same: cars whizzing by but no rides. The little food I had was dwindling, and I was getting hungry, but there were no stores around. Therefore, I walked to the next exit east, where the small town of Kimball lies. When I got there, I found a dumpster for food and ended up sleeping next to it that night.

I was completely devoid of hope, having witnessed thousands of cars pass me by. The feeling of rejection by the world was overwhelming. My parents were against me, my friends had left, and the entire population of Nebraska refused to give me a ride. Now I was eating out of a much more putrid dumpster than the fecund one at Half Moon Bay. I wept myself to sleep, broken to the farthest point I had ever found myself, literally moaning and sobbing in emotional pain. All the escapes I had made, all the running—now here was an escape I couldn't affect. I was stuck on an exit in the middle of the flatlands of the country. Stuck.

The next day I tried again to hitchhike and got nowhere. But all morning a resolve to change my life was growing inside me. I made my decision: I would humble myself and call my father for help, despite not having spoken to him in months. He no longer had the legal authority to put me in Straight, so I didn't fear that anymore. Now I needed him. I called collect from a Kimball payphone, and he agreed to help me. He would wire me funds to take the bus, but only to his home in Cincinnati and only if I stayed with him, keeping out of trouble and working a job. I agreed.

My sanity had been in dangerous territory, but it was safe now. I had a long bus ride ahead. I reflected on myself and what had transpired over the past few months. The love of nature that had begun to grow in me in the Roanoke graveyard had now gotten stronger. I didn't agree with the hippies who mooched off others; I was not a bum and did not want to be one. But I did agree with the general philosophy I learned there, that Mother Earth was sacred and that industry was harming her. Living in a redwood forest would lead almost anyone with a heart to the same conclusion. I wanted to learn more about this natural lifestyle. I also thought about my missing friend and how it was drugs that led to his mysterious disappearance. I didn't want drugs to cause such pain in my life or in others' lives. In fact, I was never to use LSD again. I felt the intense pain of rejection, loss, tragedy, and even hunger. I indeed did want to change my life as I watched the plains of Nebraska pass by through the Greyhound bus window.

25. The Green Rambler

Initially, my father was interested in seeing me succeed and hoped that I had finally had enough of the drug world. He helped me buy a car, an old 1968 American Rambler. The reverse gear didn't work, so I always had to remember to park on a hill if I needed to back up. It was a beautiful natural green, a color I began to love—the color of nature—which reminded me of melancholy. It fit me well. Looking back now, this car was symbolic of who I was at that moment: both a rambler at heart and now a green, someone in love with nature and the earth, and one with an increasingly melancholic spirit.

I quickly found a job at a local plant nursery. Things were going well. I was not using drugs. I was drinking a little but not much, and I was working full-time around plants, which I enjoyed. I met a young lady and went to visit her once. Because I came home late, my father thought I was back to my bad behavior and threw me out of the house. I got into the Rambler and left after just one month.

To this day I feel his reaction was unjustified. I didn't do anything wrong except come home an hour late. I had not been getting drunk or using drugs and was not having sex. That is not to say I would not have in the future, but at the time I was living a new and better life. Yet I can understand and sympathize with him now; he was shell-shocked from all the lies and problems I had caused him for so many years. Just the slightest error on my part was enough to convince him to boot me out. He had learned tough love through Straight and was now tougher than ever—perhaps too tough.

I headed to Virginia in the Rambler. There my brother Russell and I decided to go together to Florida. I wanted to see Key West since some of my siblings had run away there, calling it a paradise.

The solenoid of the car did not properly charge the battery, so if we stopped for gas, we had to leave the car running; otherwise, it would need a jump start. Sometimes we could shut it off if it were on a hill and then roll it down to push start it. Otherwise, the Rambler ran great.

We reached Homestead, the last major city on the mainland of Florida. I was tired, but Russell wanted to keep going. I went to sleep in the back seat as Russell continued to pound beers and drive. He eventually got tired and pulled over in Key Largo, the first island of the chain. Foolishly, he turned off the car in the middle of nowhere and passed out.

Moments later we were being attacked by swarms of mosquitoes. The car would not start, and there was no hill to push start it. There was no one around. We tried rolling up the windows to keep out the mosquitos but couldn't breathe; it was too hot and humid outside. Then we put rags in the windows, but it was still not letting enough fresh air in to breathe. Eventually, we started walking down the road to look for help, and we found a party at a houseboat and got someone to jump the car.

Instead of going further into the Keys, we decided to escape the mosquitoes by going north to Tampa. If we couldn't sleep in the car, we would have nowhere to rest since we had no money for hotels. When we got to Tampa, we parked on the beach at Treasure Island, enjoying the cool Gulf Stream breeze. We both had long hair, bell-bottom blue jeans, and redneck tans. We threw off our shirts and walked around the beach, chain-smoking our roll-your-own cigarettes. With shoes on, in full burnout regalia, we walked past bright colored preppy beachgoers, dropping their jaws.

The police showed up: "What are you guys doing here? Dumpster diving?" The officer said this since we parked near a dumpster. We had not been dumpster diving; it was only a coincidence. He said, "Show me you're IDs." We gave them, and he went to his car. When he came back, instead of leaving us alone as I expected, he said to me "You're under arrest," putting me in handcuffs, saying, "You have an outstanding warrant for driving without license, tags, or registration."

I had forgot about my arrest years earlier when I was caught driving my unregistered Chevy Impala. I had been a minor at the time but must have told the police I was an adult. My brother was free to go but not in the Rambler since he had no driver's license; his DUI had revoked it in Roanoke. The police planned to impound the car. The officer loaded me into the back seat of the police cruiser, and off I went for processing and incarceration. There was no way of escape this time.

Moments after we left, Russell (who was to tell me later) got into the car and, with his heart racing, took off. He had no money to pay the exit toll from the island so blasted through the gate. He began to drive it back north toward Roanoke.

I was booked into the Pinellas County Jail. I couldn't pay my bail, so I had to wait for a hearing. Eleven days I waited. While in jail I played card games, using cigarettes as trading currency. We slept in locked cells at night, but during the day we spent time in a common area. Once, when we were lining up to enter the mess hall to eat, a large black man in line behind me was offended that I spit on the grass. I meant him no harm; I had merely spit to my side. But he felt disrespected by this. He came around me and threw his elbow into my stomach, saying "You better respect me!" I buckled over. I felt the hardness of this place and the cold anger of those stuck in this system. I was a peace-loving person, and yet I kept finding pain and rejection. On the eleventh day, the judge ordered me released since all charges had been fulfilled or dropped.

I called my brother who had gone back to Roanoke. He said, "Sorry, man, your Rambler is gone. I abandoned it on the side of the highway in Tennessee when it ran out of gas. I didn't have money to fill the tank. I hitched home."

My lovable 1968 green Rambler was lost to me forever. I quickly forgave Russell because of all the times he had rescued me in the past. I hitchhiked to Roanoke. I went back there because it was the closest thing I had to a home. When I went to California months earlier, I hadn't left on bad terms with my mother. But I was an adult now and knew I shouldn't live in her home. But luckily, she had bought a second home on an acre of land in the Appalachian Mountains near Floyd, right off of the Blue Ridge Parkway (a beautiful, national scenic road built as part of Franklin D. Roosevelt's New Deal, winding along the spine of the Blue Ridge from the Shenandoahs to the Great Smokey Mountains). No one lived there at the time; it was meant as a family vacation home. I paid her some rent to live there as she required. It was a rustic old farmhouse, heated by a woodstove. There was electricity but no bathroom— only an outhouse.

It was a holy time for me. I was living close to the earth, void of industrial sounds and lights, under a bright sky of stars, and I was alone. I began a sort of spirituality focused on Mother Earth. My earlier cemetery meditation and my newly (Santa Cruz style) ideological love of Mother Earth started to gel into a budding, creation-oriented, earth-loving spirituality.

My brother Russell helped me to find a job near his home in Franklin County, which was close to my mountain home. I started working on the same dairy farm in Boones Mill where he worked. I wanted to be close to nature, and

I thought working on a farm was ideal. But I quickly found out that cow farms are not pristine nature. I was hired to drive a tractor around, scooping up the tons of manure, pushing it into a giant vat that was capped to create a sellable methane gas. Some cows were milked, others killed for meat, and even their refuse was sold. The cows didn't pasture full-time out on grass but were usually corralled on concrete to better control their entry and exit for milking and to easily control the flow of manure by tractor. Some of the cows were still milked, even though they were deadly sick. They would be milked no matter how fetid they looked (some were full of open sores and could barely walk). The boss told me: "As long as she's alive, she'll be milked. Even if the milk is foul, since it's mixed with a larger portion of healthy milk, it's safe enough, and we sell it."

Some employees would beat the cows with electric prods and whips, taking their full unrestrained rage out on them. I remember the tobacco chewing wads of spit flying while the electric crackling prods sparked onto cow flesh. I had seen similar cruelty to animals when I worked at the circus. These men were pure sadists who worked here, using their employment to relieve their inner violence on indefensible cows. I didn't want to work there; I couldn't even bring myself to drink their milk. I quit!

I thought a chicken farm might be better, so I had a job interview and a tour of the facility. I was shocked to find 300-foot-long barns with hallway after hallway of stacked chicken cages ten high. Thousands of chickens—each one in a small cage just enough for it to stand, without the ability to turn around. The little heads protruded out of the cages so that they could peck at food going by on a conveyor belt, and there was a separate belt taking the eggs that they dropped. The sound of one chicken is minor, but the sounds of thousands, pecking and hawing, is an intense wave of sound. And the smell: an allergic dander so acidic as to be painful entering the nose. Even trying to hold my nose didn't work—the scent could be tasted. I was born with allergies to animal dust, and I knew at that moment I would never work there, both by its outrageous treatment of chickens and the palpable offensive allergens in the air.

My time in Boones Mill and Floyd lasted just a few short months. Living in the country home was an enjoyable, even mystical experience, especially the nights of full moon, but that style of farming was incompatible with my natural, freedom-loving nature.

From my salary, I bought a hefty Honda 750, a four-cylinder motorcycle with a Windjammer fairing, as well as a backpack, tent, and guitar, and I took off on a new rambling road trip. Rambling was my new best friend. In less than a year I had bounced across the country and made it into the Keys of Florida. I had now been to over half of the States and wanted to see more.

As I rolled down the road on my motorcycle, I first returned to the home of my youth, South Lyon, to visit a childhood girlfriend. I then headed north over the magnificently long, windswept Mackinac Bridge (as my bike buffeted across its grated surface) and into the wild forests and rivers of Michigan's Upper Peninsula. I loved camping along its beautiful lakes and rivers. I didn't play the guitar well, but I enjoyed bringing it along. I felt like I was living the dream of Neil Young's album cover *Decade*: the cover image shows Neil sitting in the desert, leaning on the back of his guitar case (which was covered with stickers showing his travels), arms outstretched like Jesus on the cross.

My guitar and I traveling around America; my dream of *seeing the world* continued to come true. I kept riding west, wanting to make it to the Black Hills of South Dakota, where the massive Sturgis motorcycle rally was going on. But my motorcycle started spitting oil out of the engine, and I feared it would not get me back home. So I turned around. I began to feel disappointment; it felt as if I would always have high hopes for my adventures, but within a little while reality would come striking me across my face, halting my journey's completion. The rambling dreamer in me was not a good planner—I was discovering about myself.

But this time, instead of going back to Roanoke, my brother Patrick invited me to come live with him. He had moved to Ithaca, New York. Having to add plenty of oil to my bike along the way, I eventually made it. I arrived in early winter with my long hair and rambling ways. I would never have guessed that it was there that my life would change completely and eternally.

26. Organic Lifestyle

My brother Patrick had moved to Ithaca a few years prior and bought an old Victorian styled house, ten miles west, in the tiny village of Reynoldsville. His home—over a hundred years old—was in disrepair and needed everything. It had no running water, and the toilet was an outhouse. I took bird baths using a large basin of water I heated on the wood stove. There was no insulation, and the foundation, roof, and walls were all in need of significant repair. Sometimes in winter, the temperature would drop to negative twenty degrees Fahrenheit, and there was constant snow. It was barely livable, except in one room that had a large wood stove and some plastic covering the walls and ceiling (acting as a poor man's insulation). But there was something dynamic and vigorous about living there in such a natural state.

Patrick was (and is) four years older than me. At the time, I was nineteen, and he was twenty-three. He and I were alike in many ways. We both took more after my mother than my father. He had lived with her for many years. He was young to have already bought a house to remodel, taking after my mother in that way—both excellent at remodeling homes. He liked to smoke marijuana as I, but he never got into trouble like myself and Russell (that I am aware of). He had several hobbies that kept him busy, like grooming and breeding show dogs. He was an avid music lover, also like me. Unlike me, he was very much of an extrovert to my own introversion. He was often gone from home, spending more time with his friends at parties and various events. He had begun to be wholly devoted to the Ithaca alternative scene, having gotten a job as a waiter at the famous vegetarian Moosewood Restaurant in Ithaca. He was against the industrialization of society and entirely for the world of art and alternative living. Ithaca and the surrounding area were very left of the political spectrum—socialist and liberal or, as they would say, enlightened thinkers.

I got to know a couple that lived just up the road from my house, Preston and his wife, Candice. Preston was around thirty-years-old with bushy black hair and a beard. He was well-educated, well-read, an anti-capitalist, and an anti-industrialist. His wife Candice was not as liberally minded. She was a lawyer who worked long hours in Ithaca. She was the provider, and Preston was the stay-at-home dad to their lovely little girl named Nancy. They had moved to Reynoldsville a year earlier from Colorado (where I believe Preston had been a professor). In Reynoldsville, they bought a large house that was run down. Preston stayed home fixing it up during the day. All the rooms needed to be redone, as well as the roof and the foundation. They had a few acres of land, a cow, several chickens, and a vegetable garden. All of the milk and butter came from their cow, their eggs came from their chickens, and the vegetables from their garden. That winter, I helped Preston tap his maple trees to make delicious maple syrup—its liquid slowly dripping into large vats on the forest floor.

Preston was a loving father and faithful husband. I remember watching he and Candice take walks in the evening when she came home; the two would walk hand in hand. I admired this since I had never experienced it in my own family.

Preston believed in socialism, Marxism, and Darwinism. I learned much from him about living an alternative, natural lifestyle apart from the capitalist system. I also learned from him about Thomas Malthus and the dangers of overpopulation growth. "Overpopulation led to the industrialization of society, in turn, ruining nature," he would tell me. "Everyone should have only one child," he'd say, agreeing with the communist Chinese government's one-child policy. Much of this made sense to me as I had a great love for Mother Earth and had seen the harm of industrialization and the beauty of pure nature. I was a young apprentice learning under his tutelage.

Then there was Sebastian, who lived with Patrick and me for a few months. He was much older than my brother, but I believed he had wisdom of years. He considered himself something of a prophet, claiming to be a gypsy and spiritual medium. He had reddish-blonde hair, braided in two separate two-foot-long ponytails, with overgrown curly fingernails he refused to cut out of some spiritual belief. His face was weather worn with thick leather skin and wild eyes. He cooked all-natural food, smoked marijuana, and lived the hippie lifestyle. He was effeminate and appeared to be a homosexual but was not overly so. He had a sense of humor that was refreshing and a genuine empathy for others, even if he would flash angrily over small recurring annoyances. He always had a deck of tarot cards and believed he could learn the secrets of others through the use of them.

Meanwhile, through my brother's connections, I made several more new friends, all of whom were for a return to natural methods of agriculture and living and opposed to industrial farming. Ithaca was a hotbed of this mentality, the forerunners of the alternative lifestyle and the organic movement. It felt natural that I began to follow this movement.

That first spring I found a job that matched my newly budding ideology of alternative, natural living. It was working in the small town of Lodi on the Blue Heron organic farm, one of the earliest certified organic farms of the time. I had not heard of organic farming until moving to Ithaca, but I was quickly attracted to it as it fit my love of nature and my opposition to the outrageous farming techniques and brutality to animals I had seen.

It was hard manual work, planting and harvesting vegetables by hand, exposed to the hot sun and elements all day. But I enjoyed it, rolling around in the soil, planting potato plants and carrots by hand, and wrapping tomato vines. It gave me hours and hours to think about my life and the nature of life itself. I thought of the very essence of plant growth: plant a seed, feed and water it, watch it grow into a fruit or vegetable, and then groom the field for eventual hibernation in winter. I was reminded of sitting in the graveyard in Roanoke, stoned on marijuana, imagining from whom or what came the first tree.

All of this reflection led me to want to follow the ways of Mother Earth even more closely. I stopped trimming my beard and let it grow out thick. My hair was even longer now and packed in. My blue jeans were brown from the mud caking into them. I always wore boots and began to care not for chemical products like arm deodorant.

Being a hard worker, I got a second job at an organic bakery making bread. My boss was a man named Aron, an alternative-minded intellectual, who lived with his wife and several children in a farm home on multiple acres. The bakery was a small shed attached to their home, where three of us worked in an extremely tight space: myself, Aron, and another employee—a dreadlocked young man who called himself Me.

Most of the alternative people I had met had only one or two children—like my friend Preston—with many of them believing in the world overpopulation crisis. But Aron was different. He was living together with his wife and several children, and he wanted to be ideologically consistent in his alternative lifestyle. For example, he and his wife practiced natural childbirth, giving birth in the home without the use of any medication and with only a midwife present. From what I then understood (though it may have been more my perception than their specific ideology), they also did not believe in the use of artificial birth control. They would engage in sex, and whatever came as a result, they would accept. They thought this was in line with the way of nature, of the way of Mother Earth—the same as animals. Aron and my neighbor Preston did not get along well because of this difference in alternative lifestyle philosophy—the former for pure nature and large families and the latter for restricting population growth at home and in the world. Therefore, there was tension and animosity between the two.

For me, working at the bakery was like participating in creation. Each morning we would take a chunk of starter dough to use to make the bread. Aron had ancient sourdough starter from the Old Country where his ancestors immigrated from. His starter was a culture of dough that was supposedly hundreds of years old. The same starter would be added and grown, so it had continuity with the day before, and the day before that, etc. That starter would then rise to be able to make a new batch, and this would go on every day, week, and year, for generations.

In bread making we started with the dough, forming it in our hands—our arm muscles doing all of the work. After creating each loaf by hand, we placed them on large pans, which we then put in modern stone ovens. Midway through we would spray the loaves with water to get the crust to form just right. Then, when done, we set the bread outside to cool down on large racks. Finally, we packaged each loaf by hand in recycled cellophane wrapping. Every night I would take home at least one or two loafs for myself, and this would be one of my main staples to live on.

The bakery being attached to his home was convenient for Aron since he could watch his many kids and help his wife. Once, while we were working, his wife was having a baby in the next room. She was screaming at the top of her lungs, assisted only by a natural midwife. Aron would come to check on the baking bread and then go back to check on his wife. When the baby was born, Me and I got to see her, fresh after birth. Bread, babies, and nature, it was all lovely. It felt like the origins of creation: yeast, leaven, birth, organic, and chemical free, and there was something pristine to it all.

27. Earth First!

Aron sold the bread at a local co-op in Ithaca called Greenstar. Co-ops are a hybrid socialist-capitalist store: one purchases an annual membership, which is a share in the store's ownership. So, all the shoppers are shareholders and part owners.

Greenstar still exists today but is now a multi-million-dollar operation with multiple storefronts. Back then it was a single, small, alternative market near Thompson Park, where one could find all kinds of organic foods. It was also the go-to place for learning about alternative events and organizations, as in and around the store were flyers and politically oriented tracts. It was there I picked up my first issue of *Earth First!: The Radical Environmental Journal*, the propaganda magazine for the organization Earth First!

The central tenant of this organization was the opposition to industrialization by means of environmental terrorism. The goal was to preserve wild nature by creating havoc upon the industrialists who were exploiting her. But Earth First! was a disorganized association: the magazine provided a call to action, but there were no central meetings or common planning as such. Readers were encouraged and inspired to act in the name of Earth First! to carry out acts of radical terrorism against industrialists and developers. Earth Firsters were nicknamed *monkey wrenchers*: those who committed acts of ecosabotage.

Earth First! came to fame in 1981, when its founders unfurled a 300-foot, tapered, black sheet of plastic down onto the face of the Glen Canyon Dam in Arizona, giving it the appearance of a giant crack.[13] It was a veiled threat that it would be easy to actually set off an explosion, destroying the dam. Earth First! generated its fame by promoting the question of who would be the one to blow the dam for real, releasing the Colorado River to run free, preventing the commercialization of the land, known and believed to be sacred.

While no one had, yet, bombed any dams, many other activities were taking place, such as the cutting of fences and burning down of federally regulated National Forest land. One of the most popular activities was the metal spiking of large growth trees to scare industrialist loggers from cutting them down. If the loggers attempted to chain-saw large trees that had been spiked, their saws could hit the hidden spike and would kick back into their face, injuring them severely. If the spike went undiscovered by the logger, and the tree went to the more substantial saws in the mill, the big saws would almost certainly be ruined once hitting a spike. There was the possibility of the big saw harming the mill operator as well.

There was a debate in Earth First! as to whether a monkey wrencher should leave the spikes hidden, so that the danger was greater, or should flag the spikes to lessen the threat. By flagging them, there would be little danger to the logger or the mill operator, only the inconvenience of having to remove the spikes. I did not believe in violence or harm to others, so I thought the spikes should be flagged.

Though I never spiked any trees, I started my own independent activities, as the journal called for. I wanted to cause property harm to industrialists. I wanted to defend the natural earth against developers ruining it. In the course of about a year in Ithaca, having worked on organic farms and bakeries and having learned of this new alternative green lifestyle, this ideology of radical environmentalism had taken hold of me. It was a natural progression for me. I had started with a pure love for nature, learned the ways of hippies in California, had seen both the disgusting and cruel modern methods of farming, as well as earth-friendly organic farming techniques, and now I had found my ideology and even religion in nature. I had a mother and a planet to protect . . . and it was exhilarating.

I was so inspired I decided to build my own natural shack in the woods. The hut turned out to be entirely unlivable, however, not sealed from the rain and cold. I have an old picture of me standing next to it. There is a pained look of disappointment on my face as I knew it was a failed project, but it gave me an outlet for my new radical religion.

28. Cortés, a Killer?

Not only did I have a new religion in my environmentalism, I also had a high priest, the rock star Neil Young. Most Earth Firsters nearly worshipped him. Back in the Santa Cruz hippie camp, he was revered. It was rumored Neil lived in forests near Santa Cruz, enjoying being surrounded by people like himself, old and young hippies. In fact, when I was in Santa Cruz, some of us from the camp tried in vain to find his ranch. Neil was like a prophet at the camp. Now, as an Earth Firster, he was my prophet, too.

Neil sang as an oracle, speaking directly to the listener to influence him or her, such as his direct conversation style in the song *Days that Used to Be*, where he entreats the listener to have a one-on-one personal conversation with him. And he teaches his pliable listeners of the sacredness of nature, such as in *Mother Earth (Natural Anthem)*.

I listened to his songs for inspiration and meditation. Listening in a meditative state would cause endorphin reactions in my brain and an emotional horripilation in my body and skin. His music would, in fact, directly touch and influence my soul. One of his songs at the time fired my intellectual curiosity and would lead me to further research. It is called *Cortez the Killer* about the European explorer Hernán Cortés and his invasion of Mexico. Neil describes him as an invader and destroyer of the early Aztec's paradisal natural life. In the song, the Aztec ruler Montezuma ponders the mysteries of the world while chewing coca leaves. In this paradise the Aztecs all worked together, never hating anyone nor engaging in war. This peace-loving paradise was destroyed by Cortés who had come across the ocean with weapons of destruction.

Here was an explanation, rationale, and anthem for my new ideology. It was an outgrowth and continuation of what I learned in Santa Cruz. The Europeans came and ruined the native, sacred, and natural ways of the earth.

I had spent my teenage years admiring the beauty of creation: as a tree planter and marijuana grower and later in my reflection on the growth of trees in the Evergreen Cemetery. I hated violence and had a peace sign tattooed on my back. I had seen how industrial America was despoiling the earth with sick cow and chicken farms, and I had seen how corporate farming sadists beat animals. Our modern society had become addicted to industrial farming, which was ruining our earth and our intimacy with nature. The use of chemical insecticides was despoiling our soil and water and poisoning our bodies. There was a simple answer to all of these ills: return to organic methods of farming, free all the imprisoned animals, and return to a natural lifestyle, even one without cars and asphalt. Yes, I thought, that is the truth about mankind.

Neil Young, my oracle, was teaching me that, in fact, this paradisal world had already existed before the invasion of Christian Europeans. Cortés brought diseases and death, all for the love of gold and greed. This needed to be vindicated and reversed. This history of European industrialization appeared to be the root cause of the problem. So, I wanted to learn more about the evils of Cortés and the natural state of Aztec paradise. I went to the Ithaca library to find a book on the subject.

Perusing the bookshelf, there were a handful of books to choose from, some dated recently and one very old. I thought the best book would be the one closest in time to the actual event, rather than a book written in the past few years. The oldest book on the shelf was *Cortés, the Life of the Conqueror*, written by Francisco López de Gómara, Cortés' personal secretary. Gómara was a Catholic priest and is considered the first historian of the conquest of Mexico.[14]

To my surprise, however, as I read it, I was not learning how evil the Europeans were and how paradisiacal the natives. Instead, I began to feel sympathy for the Europeans. The book relates that when Cortés arrived in Mexico, Montezuma had many wives and slaves and was living in total opulence. He kept 3,000 women in his palace, and generally around 150 women at a time were impregnated by him, though most aborted their children since none could legally inherit. He was known to sacrifice over 20,000 living people a year and eat their flesh. Gómara writes:

> During the first days the Spaniards had arrived, whenever Montezuma went to the temple, there was the killing of men in sacrifice. To prevent such cruelty in the presence of the Spaniards . . . Cortez warned Montezuma not to sacrifice a human body, and if he did, he would devastate the temple and the city, and tear down the idols before Montezuma and all the people.[15]

Cortés spoke directly to the Aztecs, attempting to teach them why human sacrifice was not only against God but reason as well:

> Is there a man among you who wants to be killed? Indeed no. Well then, why do you kill others so cruelly? If you cannot create souls, why would you destroy them? None of you can make spirits, nor do you know how to forge bodies of flesh and bone. If you could, there wouldn't be any one of you without children. You would have as many as you wish for, and as you wanted: big, beautiful, good, and virtuous. That is given by our God of heaven; he gives those who he wants because he is God. And that's why you should take hold and worship him for who he is.[16]

I began to understand that, at least in part, Cortés and his men desired to bring integrity and peace to the indigenous Aztecs. Yes, Gómara admits some Europeans brought war and disease and were greedy for gold, silver, and precious stones. But the natives were not as peace-loving as Neil described them; instead, they would amp up their bodies while killing their own in bloody sacrifices, where blood would flow like a river down the steps of the sacred temple. The temple entrance itself was designed like an entrance to hell: a painted serpent's mouth, open with exposed fangs. Inside the temple were walls blackened with dried blood, and stench emanating from the flesh of sacrificed babies and virgins.

I thought that this indigenous practice of sacrifice was far more fanatical than the European religion Christianity. To me, the Aztecs appeared to be murderers. Murder is the taking of a life without just cause, the destruction of innocent life. Of course, I thought one must know that murder is wrong for it to be so, and perhaps their society did not believe it as wrong. Yet the human heart knows better. How could it not be wrong? Every man and woman (and even animals) believes in his or her own right to exist; no one wants to be killed. It is a natural right, and the Aztecs violated it, I thought.

Neil Young didn't see this as a violation of natural rights, but instead just an alternative and legitimate way of life. He sang that the Aztecs would offer up lives in sacrifice so that the society itself could continue. But after reading Gómara's book, I began to see how inconsequential Neil's lyrics were. Really? The paradisiacal culture allowed, or even mandated, the killing of others so the society could continue? That's absurd, I thought.

But the book did not change me. I did not reject Neil Young's music to pursue a different ideology. It's only a song, I thought. Instead, the book planted tiny seeds in my mind: a seed of doubt about the natural paradise of man and a grain of respect for the European civilization that helped tame human sacrifice.

Today, in our era that often exalts nativism over culture, Cortés is almost universally condemned. Some of the criticism may be fair. Looking back now, perhaps my positive feelings toward Cortés were due to the talented author Gómara's wordsmithing.[17] It didn't hurt, too, that I had a great love of exploration and found that Cortés had this same mirific love. I had more in common with him than with the Aztecs. Cortés wanted to see the world; so did I.

29. A Grand European Tour

It was a quiet life in Reynoldsville, reading books and working on farms. To have fun, I would drive to Ithaca. Even though I was underage, I would go to the bars using a fake ID. There, usually at a bar called the Chanticleer, I would play pool with many students who were attending Cornell and Ithaca College. I would hear them talk, not only about their classes but about their summer travel ideas—most of them were planning to go to Europe. They were educated young people and appeared to be happy. They were like me in that they had a love of travel and adventure—they too dreamt of seeing the world. But they were unlike me in that they were studying for their future. I had never met people like this before: they smoked marijuana and drank, but were studious and well-traveled.

I had defined myself as a druggie and a high school dropout. Growing up, there were only two categories I was familiar with: the jocks and the burnouts. I never fit either category entirely since I was also into art, but I ended up following the burnout style more closely because I used drugs (and experimented with the thoughts in my mind). Straight, Inc. had reinforced in me the idea that *once a druggie always a druggie.* I categorized myself this way. But here was a new category that impressed me. Of course, I knew that most of these kids came from well-off families, so I could differentiate (or minimize) them, but I admired their desire for travel to Europe and their education.

Hearing the students talking about visiting Europe struck me as something I could do. Gómara's book on Cortés gave me even more reasons to visit Europe, notably Spain and Portugal, where the first New World explorers came from. And who else lived in Spain but my two friends, Blythe and Lucía. Perhaps I could see them again. Having worked multiple jobs all summer, I now had some money saved up. My job on the organic farm was coming to the end of the season, so I decided I would go to Europe for a month or two. None of my family had ever been to Europe. I would be the first.

I headed there in October of 1989. I was twenty years old. I utilized a form of air hitchhiking called Airhitch. It was a very cheap way to get to Europe and back. The only drawback was that I could not plan the exact date and destination of travel. I had to have a one-week open window of time to be ready to fly, and I could not choose the precise destination. When I was ready, I would let Airhitch know, and they would inform me of the destination and the exact date of departure from New York City. I called, and they told me that I would fly out in a few days and would arrive in Copenhagen, Denmark.

My journey started at the Eastern Airways terminal at New York's JFK Airport. It was virtually empty, and there was rain coming in from the ceiling. Eastern had just declared bankruptcy so had completely let go of taking care of the terminal. It did not inspire confidence, and I was already very nervous since I had never flown before.

On the flight, I chain-smoked because of my nerves. But my seat row was fourth from the rear, and only the final three rows had ashtrays where smoking was allowed. As I smoked, I doused my cigarettes in a foam cup filled with a little water. In turn, I received many dirty looks from passengers; a long-haired kid, chain-smoking and dousing butts in a water cup on an airplane, is no way to impress.

The plane landed early morning, and I was immediately in culture shock. There was no English anywhere. I had no idea what I was doing or where I was going. Again, as was my life's *modus operandi*, I would jump first and then discover I lacked any plan. But luckily the train station was very near to the airport. I spent several hours trying to figure out what to do; it seemed no one wanted to help me. I received dirty looks from everyone. I had to calm down and become oriented.

When I did so, I first went into the city to view a famous statue called the Little Mermaid. Since I was uneducated, I had no idea what the significance of it was or why a mermaid was so famous. Later I would learn that the Little Mermaid statue was based on the fairy-tale of the same name, written by the famous Danish author Hans Christian Andersen. The figure was wrought out of bronze by Edvard Eriksen in 1913 and depicts the mermaid sitting on a rock.

I didn't know any history of Europe at the time, having dropped out of high school. One person I met said to me, "You are foolish for having come to Europe without knowing any of its history." I was seeing things of great importance but had little idea of their significance.

I returned to the train station now worrying about where to sleep as it was getting late.

I brought my backpack and camping gear with me. My entire budget was minimal, $350. I had no money for hotels. I remembered my bartender friend Charley from Roanoke who had told me he had free-camped in castles throughout Europe. I imagined it was easy to free-camp. But now it didn't seem as easy as I imagined. I didn't know where any of these castles were or how to find them: I felt like a fool. Act first and think later describes who I was.

Eventually, I boarded a train going into the countryside, figuring I would get off when I saw a castle or a wooded area where I could camp. In my train car, there were a group of about five school-age kids, carrying books and homework, but who were drinking and some drunk. Supposedly, the drinking age in Denmark was only sixteen at the time. As I saw it then, this liberal law seemed like a good idea. Yes, these kids were drinking and drunk, but the whole group was still in school and was sticking together helping one another. This was eye-opening in that here there was more legal freedom to do what you wanted but more responsibility and camaraderie. Growing up, I felt that I had to choose to be either all bad or all good. I could not be a good friend, helpful, and stay in school and at the same time drink and sometimes get drunk. Instead, if I got drunk, I was branded a bad boy, which is the branding I had accepted about myself. I could now see a new way, and I was a bit sad I had never learned this new way before. Why had I thrown away my education to be this bad boy? I could have been both, like these youths seemed to be. The dichotomy I had long imagined was not necessarily real.

After getting lost on the train, I finally made it to the village of Fakse. I deboarded and walked around until I found a hedgerow with a line of trees. I couldn't put up my tent since the wind felt like gale force, and I was worried local farmers would see the bright tent in the morning. So, I slept inside my sleeping bag, wrapped up in my unassembled tent as my stuff spun around in the wild wind. It was a cold night, and thorn bushes surrounded me. Due to jet lag, I slept until noon the next day. My bright rolled up tent did not get me noticed, even though the tractors were running in the fields nearby. Or maybe I had been seen but left alone.

Over the next few days, I went south to Stege and crossed by ferry into Puttgarden, Germany. There I stopped in a local pub since I was legal age to drink, which was eighteen I believe. Some local patrons took a liking to the novelty of an American youth in their bar and bought me several shots of

Jagermeister. We played quarters with shot glasses, and one patron invited me to stay at his place for a few nights. His name was Folken. He was the manager of the Resi-Rock Discothek, a rock revival club. Folken was an odd man living with his girlfriend. He surprised me when he said, "Aliens have recently landed on the planet," and later saying that, "The German government has too many socialist laws and has become tyrannical." It was a strange place. Folken said all the homes in Puttgarden could only be painted a particular color. It was true: I had not seen such uniformity of color before. The German government did appear to be overbearing when compared to the hodgepodge of house colors back home.

I continued south by hitchhiking toward Hamburg. A sheep farmer gave me a ride to the outskirts of the city where he lived on a farm with his family. He told me the socialist government was essentially paying him to start a farm. I thought this a novel concept as I had never heard of this before. He too invited me to stay a few days.

On the plane from New York, I had met Karen—a girl my age, a beautiful, lily-white German, with a full head of flowing blonde hair, and blue eyes. She had given me her address, and said, "If you ever come to Hamburg, you can stay at my flat a few days." Well, there I was, and yes, of course, I would go. My sheep farmer friend gave me a ride to her place. I stayed there a few days with her and her roommates.

One evening she brought me to a local techno club. Inside, everything was wrapped in cellophane, and blue lights pulsated all around. People were dressed in electronica fashion as it was the trend all over the city. I was standing in my dirty boots with my flannel shirt and long hair, looking entirely out of place. My eyes were wide open trying to take in this strange world. It felt like the world I had once admired of David Bowie, closer to who I had been as a cross-dressing youth. It was so much different than the new me: the green hippie, the druggie, the Earth Firster.

The next day, during one of my solo expeditions in the city, I wandered into a place called the Reeperbahn and saw a group of people trying to enter a blocked-off street. Curious what was there I followed them into the infamous Herbertstrasse. Walking down the street, I first saw white towels lying on chairs inside a building and thought it was some salon. But as I continued I saw women trying to sell sex. I would find out that the Herbertstrasse is a street where prostitution is tolerated.

The area smelled of chemical and tobacco, and there were dirty old men wandering about. I went inside one place called Lady Lyn, where Asian women were lying on top of men, though still dressed. I began to feel depressed. I was afraid of falling into this behavior myself, and I did not want that.

Something inside me had changed. When I first moved to Ithaca, I began engaging in sexual activity as often as I could find a girlfriend. I dated several women, including some much older than me. My ideas of nature and organics seemed to mix easily with frequent natural sex. But I wasn't a wild animal for commercial lust, as I had seen in the Herbertstrasse. I didn't want to fall into the desire of sex for money. It seemed dirty. I had once hired a prostitute in my early teenage days, and it left me feeling empty and full of despair. I would not do this again.

While I did desire to be with Karen, I also wanted just to be her friend. Something in Europe calmed me. When I got back to her flat, I told Karen about what I had seen that day and how I felt about it. She and I talked long hours about the needs of young people, of love and reality, in a platonic way, and I enjoyed every moment of it.

I thought about staying with Karen longer, but I felt my time was over and I needed to move on. We were so different, too; she was clean and preppy, and I was a long-haired hitchhiker, who wasn't using deodorant out of ideology. I wondered why she gave me such a warm welcome. Her optimistic outlook must have seen something authentically attractive behind my hippie facade, or she was simply a charitable person.

While in Hamburg I heard that the Berlin Wall had recently fallen and that both sides of Berlin could now be visited. I decided to go. To get to Berlin, the train still had to cross the formerly communist East Germany. At the time, the tracks in East Germany were terrible so the train would slow to just thirty miles per hour for the entire trip. I remember looking out the window in West Germany as the train sped along at eighty miles per hour, past the clean and organized countryside with its modern cars and buildings. Then, immediately upon crossing into East Germany, everything was dirt poor—old cars were everywhere, and its rough roads and train tracks were falling apart. It took forever on the train, and I began to regret going.

Finally, I reached Berlin. West Berlin was just like West Germany, modern and beautiful. I walked through the city, under the Brandenburg Gate, and onto the ground where the wall had fallen. I had imagined a big wall separating the two sides, but instead, it was a large strip of land with fencing on both sides, and the wall was in the middle. By now though, the wall and most of the fences had been taken down, leaving the entire zone abandoned and dead looking— no grass growing, just dirt, rocks, and cement. I walked without restriction on this wide strip of land. There were old, rundown, abandoned buildings inside the empty zone. I wandered into what I recall was a small church but may have just been a small building. A homeless man was living inside. Graffiti quoting Karl Marx was sprayed on the walls in English: *Religion is the opiate of the people.* I just then remembered my neighbor Preston in Reynoldsville, who believed this philosophy of Marx. He had explained to me that religion promotes the false dream of a paradise in the afterlife, which creates a moral hazard and prevents mankind from building a heaven on earth. It seemed real to me then.

I left Berlin and headed west by overnight train. I had bought a Eurail pass that allowed me to travel by train for a few twenty-four-hour periods over the course of a month. So, whenever I took a train, I tried to make sure it was as long as possible to get the maximum of my twenty-four hours and a good night's sleep inside the train, while reclined in my seat (or, if possible, lying on the floor). Therefore, I chose to go to Amsterdam, Netherlands, on the night train, a long ride.

When I arrived, I felt as if I had landed on another planet. Back in the U.S., I had been put into the Straight rehab and chased by police for smoking marijuana; now I was in a city where marijuana and hash were legally sold in shops. It was a paradise, I thought. Buying hash was as easy as buying a cup of coffee. My first visit to the city was to one of its cafés. It was an excellent place, full of art and light, not a seedy drunken bar. I went in, ordered a cup of coffee and some golden hashish, and I sat there, drinking my coffee and smoking hash, feeling a sense of freedom and of beating the system of a repressed America . . . as smoke wafted through the air.

The entire city was breathing and alive. Everywhere I walked I could smell the natural drug. It was not hippies or burnouts I saw, but well-dressed gentlemen walking down the street, smoking it out of distinguished looking pipes. They were not walking slowly and aimlessly; rather they were on their way to work and milling about. It was a strange new world in a very old one.

At the tourist office, I met a Canadian girl my age who, like me, was backpacking Europe on her own. We enjoyed the entire day together, walking arm in arm, exploring the city. Trolleys, bikes, cars, buses, and pedestrians—all buzzing about in a chaotic but organized way. Waterways, houseboats, coffee houses, and tall apartment buildings—all jammed into a small city among canals. There were markets everywhere with beautiful, embroidered, Moroccan-style clothing for sale. Women wore the most strikingly colorful scarves (something I had never seen in the U.S. before). There were lusciously large tulips for sale throughout the city. My mother would have been in heaven seeing such plants. The city felt like a living work of art. I found it the most intriguing city in Europe that I had seen.

At the end of the day (unlike me), my new Canadian friend went to her hotel and was to leave the city the next morning. Since I could not afford a hotel, I spent the night sleeping on the beach in nearby Zandvoort. I crawled up under a boardwalk, nestling into the soft but cold sand, and tried to sleep as a bone-chilling wind blew.

The first day had been one of the happiest days of my life, but the second day would be much worse. My beautiful friend was gone, and I began to see things that disgusted me. As I was walking around, I saw a young man dumpster diving. He looked like a complete animal without rationality. The word *man* did not even seem to define him. He smelled of rancid feces and was not just digging in the dumpster but was devouring whatever trash he found with wide-open jaws, spilling fluids from his mouth all about. I thought, was this the seedy underbelly to the legalization of drugs? Perhaps those raised well could continue to use drugs and live a productive life, but was this the fate of those not so fortunate?

I continued rambling around and wandered into the De Wallen, a legal prostitution area. There were gates of entry into the pedestrian walkway, and right away I saw the red neon lights beaming out from the large storefront windows. As in Hamburg, the women were showing off their bodies and attempting a negotiation with the men passing by for sex. The women were gorgeous, unlike the worn-out girls from the Herbertstrasse. I quickly learned, however, that the window women were, in fact, models, not prostitutes. They negotiate outside and then send the men inside to meet their not-so-attractive lovers.

I remembered not only the Herbertstrasse but the same type of little wiry and ugly men back in Juarez, Mexico, years earlier: seedy, bent-over, with darkness beaming from their eyes, walking around as if entirely controlled by an animalistic demon inside them called lust. As in Mexico, Asmodeus was alive and well in Europe as well.

My second and third nights in Amsterdam had become grueling. I could not afford a hotel, there were no cheap hostels, and there were no wild spaces for camping. I ended up sleeping on a park bench my second night, and the third night I slept in a car someone had graciously allowed me to crawl into.

Finally, late the next day, I hitched a ride to Paris, going through Belgium. I was able to sleep in the car, but I was restless with wild dreams, thinking about my life of running, bouncing around, all my failed relationships with women, and how I desired the stability and joys of true love. Depressed thoughts began to fill my mind.

My ride dropped me on the outskirts of Paris, near the subway. Since I hadn't slept well the past few nights, I was cranky, and it was pouring rain. I had no place to sleep, Paris was too expensive, and the rain prevented me from touring the day on foot.

In my testiness, I decided to avoid Paris and go to the countryside to camp. I spent several hours riding in the subway, trying to find a way to the far eastern outskirts of Paris, near the rural highways. I was dirty, and I smelled for lack of a shower (it had been nearly a week). My hair was long and unwieldy, but I began to tie it in a ponytail to better fit in with the more cleanly look of Europeans. My backpack and boots were full of mud. As I was sitting on the subway, fashionably dressed men and women entered and egressed, looking at me with disgustful eyes. This was my first experience of the Parisian people, thinking them to be fashionably proud and humanly rude. I've always been a sensitive person, having an artistic nature. These sort of looks hurt me; I wanted to curl up and disappear.

These irritants reached a high level, and my spirits were sullen. I felt like going home. All the prostitution everywhere, lack of sleep, and the animal living in the dumpster. I was sick of it. I too was an animal in the way the French looked at me, in the way I saw myself, and in contrast with the clean and beautiful Karen in Hamburg. What had I become? I had no money for hotels, and all the fabled castles I searched for were nowhere to be found; instead, I was sleeping on beaches, in cars, and on park benches. My unwashed hippie ways were out of sync in Europe. I was ready to fly back to New York.

The rain let up late in the day as I reached the eastern terminus of the subway. I decided to continue my journey, hoping my luck would change. I started hitchhiking east toward Germany. Suddenly, an old Citroën pulled up, and an elderly couple offered me a ride to Nancy, France, where they lived. Neither spoke a syllable of English, and I spoke nothing in French, but we communicated through hand gestures and by drawing pictures on my notepad. When we arrived in Nancy, they invited me into their home and introduced themselves as Monsieur and Madame Gilbert Houlliere. Their son had grown up and moved out to attend school, so they had an extra bedroom for me to stay in.

Madame Houlliere asked me (using several hand gestures) to leave my boots in the garage, along with all my gear and clothes. I took a long-desired shower while she prepared a fantastic dinner of chicken, noodles, bread, cheese, salad, and horseradish. Monsieur Houlliere drank an entire bottle of wine during the meal, informing me that in France wine is used in place of water. It was my first experience of dining with an old-world European family.

After dinner, clean, with a full stomach, and relaxed by the wine, I retired to my room. It was a simple, small room with only a dresser and one large bed with a beautiful royal red bedspread. Nothing more was in the room, except that above the headboard was a large crucifix around eighteen inches long. It was a traditional wood cross with a lifelike bloody Jesus, hanging there in pain but with purpose. I laid down on that soft bed in total comfort, my body having been worn out and tired from sleeping in cars and on park benches. Lying my head on the pillow, my eyes naturally fell upward upon the calm crucifix above me. There I lay in total peace, feeling the love emanating from the home, as I quickly fell asleep.

I slept in very late and enjoyed a bountiful breakfast in the morning. The Houllieres then surprised me with more kindness. They had not only washed all my clothes but had cleaned my tent and boots as well. They had been filthy with stink and mold due to my nearly a month of European rambling. They also prepared a large bag of food for me to take on my journey. Finally, the lovely couple drove me a few miles from town and dropped me on the eastbound highway. I felt sad leaving them. They had shown so much kindness to me.

Monsieur and Madame Houlliere did not know me and could not communicate with me. I must have appeared to them as some strange, out-of-place alien in the rural countryside of Lorraine, France. In the past, I was a drug user, a dealer, a thief, a radical environmentalist, and now an unwashed hippie. Yet, this kind Catholic couple was willing to provide me with a place to stay and a meal fit for a king without their getting anything in return from me, not even the pleasure of a pleasant conversation. I will always remember them and that crucifix hanging above the bright red bed.[18]

30. A Miracle in Freiburg

My spirits were much higher now, and I was ready to continue the trip. I made my way to Strasbourg in Alsace, France. I stopped in a church, where I had heard that a priest served pea soup to those in need. It was a delicious meal from a generous man. Meeting the priest and the Houllieres in quick succession had impressed me, and I had a fleeting moment where I imagined perhaps I needed religion.

But the thought dissipated quickly. During the meal, I met a man who called himself a Catholic, who gave me a ride south. As we rode, he began telling me of his cheating on his wife with another woman. I had a bad feeling about him and asked that he drop me off. The loving marital home I had experienced in Nancy was contrasted with the cheating of this man. My newly warm feelings toward religion got a little colder. But also, more importantly, I was not ready to give up my pocket full of hash from Amsterdam.

I made my way across the German border and into the city of Freiburg im Breisgau. The vibrant city with old cobblestone streets had an immense, lofty, majestic cathedral in the middle of town, called the Freiburg Minster. I had never seen a church this big, old, and grand. It was built in Gothic style in the 1200s. It is considered to have the most beautiful spire on earth, one of the few from the Middle Ages to have survived the wars, almost entirely intact, and bursting with intricate detail. It can be seen for miles in every direction. On and around the church were several references to astrology, including an enormous clock with zodiac symbols. This was odd to see since I had remembered my father teaching me that astrology was a sin because it opposed religion. Perhaps my father didn't know as much history as he thought. There were hundreds of statues of saints and demons carved into the stone structure. The faith of the builders could not be ignored. I could imagine the level of passion and mysticism that went into building it by hand. Looking at it was like being on an LSD trip—but something much more profound, gentler, and thought-provoking, bridging my mind to a long-lost age, nearly a thousand years past.

I enjoyed walking around the city of Freiburg, but it seemed the only things to see other than the cathedral were commercial shopping venues. After all of my work on organic farms and my worship of Mother Earth, I had no love for commercialism. I was ready to leave after the first day, but there was a snag. Before I left for Europe, I took half of my travel money with me, $175. The other $175 I left in New York with my neighbor Preston to send me when I needed it.[19] I had only a few dollars left, so I called Preston and asked him to wire my money to the post office in Freiburg. The post office clerk told me, "You have to wait a few hours before the money will be available." So, while waiting, I spent the rest of my money on a nice meal.

But when I returned to the post office the money was not there. The clerk said, "Come back and try tomorrow." I had no money left, and nowhere to sleep in that urban environment. I was stuck having to wait. With nowhere to go, I went to the police station to ask for help. They referred me to a homeless shelter where I was given a bed. It was dirty, loud, and full of drunks, but I slept.

The next morning, I went back to the post office, but the money was still not there. I called Preston, and we discovered the problem. He accidentally wired the money to another Freiberg, omitting the "im Breisgau." The money went to the wrong location. The clerk informed me that, "Your money will be delayed and will come in about three days."

I couldn't go back to the homeless shelter because a bed was allowed only one night per week. I called the U.S. Consulate, but they couldn't help me for several days. I was distraught. So, I went to the only place a person could go to find respite in the city, the Freiburg Minster.

I went inside to sit, and there I remained for hours and hours. I did not go there to pray since I never prayed to the Christian God. I went there because there was no place else to go to wait out the day. But my heart was slowly turning to God in my need. I felt sad, alone, and dejected. I had nothing. I began to cry and wonder why this was happening to me. I put my head in my hands and just waited out the day, wondering where I would sleep the next few nights. I was in the middle of the city and had no money for food or transport to the mountains where I could camp.

As I sat there moping with no plan, a man walked up to me, leaning toward me, and speaking in German. I didn't understand him. I tried to answer in English, but he didn't comprehend me. He then began to use hand gestures to get his point across. He started to point at the locked money box where parishioners donated to the church. Then he pointed at me. What was he trying to say? For me to steal from the money box? No, he took out fifty Deutschmarks (then equivalent of about twenty-five dollars) and waved at me to have it. I understood that he was telling me that he was giving this money to me instead of the church—that his gift to the church was going to be a gift to me. I had no idea why he was doing this. I did not ask anyone for money. I made no signs that I needed money. I had scammed for money once, under the tutelage of Greg during our ramble to California, but since then had never done it again. I was merely sitting there with my backpack, ponytail, and dirty boots in a somber, downcast mood. My crying was not loud or noticeable. I was internalizing my problems. I was not praying, I thought, but I was speaking to God, questioning why.

I could not help but think this was a real miracle. I needed money badly but had no inclination to ask for any. Somehow this man knew that I needed money. Now I had fifty Deutschmarks. Was this God helping me?

I left the Minster in a gleeful daze, immediately going to the local grocery store, where I bought food to last for three days, as well as chocolate and a two-liter bottle of wine (which substantially weighed down the load in my backpack). I then made my way out of town to the nearby Black Forest, where I would camp out for the next few nights. How fate turns, I thought.

As I was leaving town, I had to pass by the Minster again, and there I saw a small commotion in the outside square. A man was standing on a soapbox, holding up a book, yelling out what appeared to be prophecies, with a small group circled around him. One person in that small group was a lovely young lady handing out flyers, who looked to me like an angel. She had on a pure white, flowing, lacy dress with a matching translucent mantilla that covered her tight, curly, brown locks. There was a mysterious and pure quality to her. I took one of her flyers so as to meet her. She spoke English, and we started a conversation. She introduced herself as Esther, saying, "That man on the soapbox is my father, he is citing Scripture, warning passersby about the dangers of hell, and extolling them to turn their lives to Christ, to become Bible-believing Christians." "Oh, I see," I said, taken back. It was hard to imagine this beautiful and magnetic girl was the daughter of such a stern-looking man, saying sort-of absurd things, I thought. But she was so cute that I didn't care so much. We spoke for a while and exchanged addresses. I would have liked to get to know her, but I needed to get out of town for a few days to camp.

I spent the next few days in the pine tree picturesque Black Forest in Baden-Württemberg. I had the happiest heart, walking, camping, eating chocolate, and drinking wine. Over my course there, I would hike the twenty-five miles to the top of Mt. Feldberg at nearly 5,000 feet. After passing many small Christian shrines along the trail (something that I had never seen in any U.S. public spaces), I arrived at the peak, with its views into Germany, France, and Switzerland. I saw there the great snow-capped mountains of the Swiss Alps far south on the horizon. There was not a wisp of haze in the sky to cloud the view. There were clouds, but they were below, looking like a white ocean between me and that wondrous range. It felt as if I were looking at an artistic masterpiece, created by the God of nature's own hands.

As I sat there drinking my bottle of wine—that fruity bouquet of happiness, I just then remembered Sebastian from Ithaca. Before I left, he gave me a tarot card. He said I could communicate with him through it. I didn't believe in mediums, but out of love of friendship, I poured some of the wine onto the card in an oblation of friendship.

My time in the forest was mesmerizing. I didn't want to return to the post office, but I knew I had to. And yes, the money was there waiting for me. My mood was high, but I didn't want to have to suffer sleepless nights anymore, rambling about and feeling out of place and rejected as I had begun to feel in Amsterdam and Paris. So, I decided instead to make my final destination to Spain.

I called Airhitch, and they found me a flight a week later out of Madrid. I had not spoken to my friend Lucía in two or more years, but I had her phone number and hoped it still worked. I sat in a call center and dialed her. To my surprise, she came on the phone. My heart was fluttering; I felt so lucky. I told her I had a flight out of Madrid back to New York in about a week. To my surprise, she said, "You should come and stay with my family for the week." I asked if Blythe was in town as well, but she told me she had lost touch with her after she moved back to Ibiza. I, too, had lost touch with her.

I saluted the Black Forest goodbye, gave thanks to the Freiburg Minster, and boarded the overnight train. I was off to Spain and was as excited as a schoolboy to see my friend.

31. Dignity in Europe

When I arrived at the Madrid railway station, I had to wait several hours for Lucía to pick me up. So, I walked about the city (over ten miles), gazing at all the people and architecture. The city was frenetic and sometimes dirty. Many people were sleeping in the streets, and there were thousands of cars oozing thick and foul pollution. There were men in business suits and young caballeros with cigarettes dangling out of their mouths as they flew by on mopeds—looking like James Dean. Now I understood why Lucía was so comfortable riding on the back of my Piaggio moped when no other girls I knew would be caught doing that in Roanoke. I walked past a chaotic memorial of hundreds of chairs piled up high in a fountain near Barclays Bank and saw posters everywhere of a Spanish communist who had died just days earlier.[20] Ceremonies and protests were taking place all over the city.

There was violence in the air, too. I walked past several military men in uniform with machine guns. They sternly looked directly at me as if they were ready to shoot. I wasn't doing anything. I had no idea what was going on. I had never seen anything like this in the U.S. I just kept walking. As I did so, I could not help but notice that everywhere I went were large outdoor murals of my favorite artist, Joan Miró. I had only seen lithographs from him in the small art studio near my home as a youth, and here entire city buildings were draped in my favorite form of art, surrealism: the free-flowing of shapes in the mind, created through the hand.

Lucía finally arrived. She was still stunning with wavy curls of brownish-black hair and darkened Spanish skin, thin and fashionable. She was as fun as ever. She picked me up in her small car, and we drove north about an hour to her family home in La Moraleja. She was attending university now and had a boyfriend. It was clear there was not going to be anything more than a friendship still, but it didn't matter since my admiration for her was too great to be jealous.

As we drove to her home, the highway was completely backed up for miles. But Lucía was not one to take things patiently and in stride. Instead, she wheeled her car onto the shoulder illegally and sped along at a high rate of speed for several miles as we passed thousands of other vehicles just sitting there. Sometimes we had to turn up into the grass to get around them. This was the frenetic, fun Lucía who I remembered. As soon as we saw the flashing lights of the police, she swerved back into the car lane. There were dozens of police with sirens everywhere, but we were not caught in our illegal shoulder-driving as they were too busy with some crisis, which I would learn about later.

We finally arrived at her elegant, upper-middle-class home. Her mother and father were relatively young and both attractive. Her sisters were all very natural and beautiful as well. She had no brothers. It was a new experience for me to stay with an intact family for a few days. Here was a mother and father still in love, sharing a home and family together—something I had rarely experienced. Few of my friends had both a mother and father in the home.

Lucía's mother made traditional Spanish Paella the first night. We would then have delicious meals together the entire week. Her mother was an artist like my mother. I admired her artwork as well as many famous reproduced prints in the home. To my surprise, there was a large crucifix hanging prominently in the living room. I remembered my father's house with the one faded painting of St. Anthony in the Desert and a cross in his room but nothing else, just plain drab walls—in comparison to my mother's house of rich art in every corner. Lucía's home was a harmonious confluence of my two worlds that I had thought were diametrically opposed: my father's Catholicism and my mother's art. It was eye-opening to see the two worlds united. I had never known Lucía was raised a Catholic until now. I had left that religion I was forced into when I was ten years old, and now I was seeing it throughout Europe, and in the homes of those I admired.

The next morning Lucía and I went to a large, open-air street market near the El Retiro Park. There she helped me pick out some new clothes to wear: a black, long-sleeve shirt with Miró style swirls of color. Being around Lucía made me want to look my best. Only my mother and Lucía could get me to dress well. I had forgotten about the times I would look nice for her when we went out in Roanoke. So much had changed in the past few years: I had become a full-blown, earth-loving hippie. I no longer had any nice artistically styled clothes to impress her. Those days had long passed, and now I looked like a tree growing in the woods.

Unlike my parents, hers were very well traveled, having been to many countries. They believed that travel helped a person to develop culture and the mind. This is why they sent their seventeen-year-old daughter to live in

Virginia for a year. I had never understood that before: why someone from cultured Europe would live in backwater Roanoke. It made utter sense to me now as I loved to travel as well and could easily understand how it expanded my own mind.

Later that week, while watching television, I learned that both of the police incidents I had seen my first day in Madrid were related. The soldiers I had seen with machine guns had been looking for a Basque separatist, who had entered a government building and assassinated a government official.

The Basque were then (and still are) an indigenous ethnic group in northern Spain, who have their own language and traditions but have never had their own nation. Some were terrorists, according to the Spanish government, since they bombed and killed to gain their independence.

The second incident, where the police had nearly closed the highway on the way to Lucía's house, was due to another Basque separatist incident, where a sniper on a hill had shot into a car, killing a government official. Madrid was undergoing all-out terrorist warfare from the Basque breakaway movement. The Basque separatists were not unlike Earth Firsters, I thought, in that they believed in using terrorism to achieve their goals. But murder went too far for me!

I spent much of my time alone the next few days as Lucía was in school or with her boyfriend. During this time I visited several museums, including the Del Prado. I walked with open eyes, open mind, and an awestruck heart, gazing at the magnificence of it all, taking in so many lessons of history and morality through the paintings. I found myself unable to pull my eyes away from a 500-year-old painting by Hieronymus Bosch, entitled *The Garden of Earthly Delights* (c. 1490–1510). It is a triptych, including panels of creation and the next life. The first panel is of Adam and Eve in the garden of paradise with a youthful God, looking like Jesus and holding the hand of a naked, pure, white-skinned Eve, who is adorned with flowing, blonde locks. Adam is seated on the left of God with the tree of life looming behind. In the middle panel is what appeared to me to be a bacchanal festival, seemingly representing a paradisiacal heaven. It is the garden of pure delight with various human races and animals of all kinds, feasting and lovemaking, dancing and living in total freedom, and seeking various forms of pleasure. This heaven had a physicality that I could relate to. I had seen other representations of heaven before—

usually showing pure angels singing before God. This never appealed to me. But Bosch's creatures living total liberation did. The painting resonated with me since I was a very carnal person and could understand a heaven that was full of earthly beauty and pleasure. The panel on the right shows hell with its wars and destruction, its contorted men, women, and animals in excruciating pain. Wild beasts are attacking and eating humans. It appears to show the result of sexual predation. There is something like a giant white satanic figure in the middle—a sort of central controlling figure. If this were in any way true, it would be a terrible place to end up, I thought.

It is a fascinating work, mixing surrealism with Christianity. I was learning more about surrealism. It was a movement that had begun at the turn of the twentieth century, influenced by Sigmund Freud's ideas of the conscious mind repressing the power of the imagination: setting the mind free from consciousness imparts its real potential. Yet, Bosch was a Christian painter, who seemed to have discovered surrealism nearly half a millennium earlier and had never been given credit.

My brain was spinning as my eyes stared at several more religious paintings. *The Descent of the Cross* by Rogier van der Weyden (c. 1435) shows a gracefully limp Mother Mary, having fainted, as Jesus's body is being lowered from the cross. Throughout the museum were many paintings of heaven and hell and the Last Judgment; terribilita everywhere: sinners being pulled into the fiery ground by demons. Yet there was the glory of the saints being lifted to the heavens by angels. The ancient artists were teaching lessons about morality and its consequences. I had remembered a Bible quote as a child, that hell is reserved for foul sinners, *where there is darkness, and where there will be wailing and grinding of teeth*. I couldn't help my emotions from being tweaked by such imagery. I was not immune to fear of the unknown and afterlife. I knew there was kindness in the world, and I knew there was evil. What followed this life? Would there be a judgment to reward the former and punish the latter? It seemed a reasonable concept based on the idea of justice.

My week in Madrid was ending as was my entire European adventure. There was one word that I felt then as the primary lesson of my trip: *dignity*. I thought that I had lost dignity in life. I had little as a full-blown hippie, and I wondered if I had ever really had much of it. Woods, earth, and animalism were my new virtues, not civility, refinement of character, education, and the like. The only times I remembered having a feeling of dignity was when I was trying to please Lucía. I didn't seem to care otherwise.

I had been grungy, dirty, unfashionable, and uneducated. I wanted to change; I wanted a new level of refinement. And I also began to reflect on the idea of religion again, of needing some kind of faith to be a more dignified person. The kindest, most loving people whom I had met had that one thing in common, faith.

It was time to say my farewell to Lucía. I was the luckiest man to have seen her again, but I felt sad upon leaving. She had been a sort of role model for me in Roanoke: she had never used drugs, was a bright, beautiful friend who was pure, not cavorting with men and bad influences. But now I had learned, she had started to (minimally) use drugs, hash especially, and seemed to have regret or conflict with her boyfriend. That gleam in her eye was now dimming. Outwardly I did not judge her though, and thought to myself it was normal, but deep inside it made me sad.

I have never seen or heard from Lucía again, having lost touch with her. But I still remember her: the wild cowlick in her hair, her beauty, her fun-loving attitude toward life, and her artistic style. I'm sure I will never see her again in this life, but her memory lives inside me. And honestly, that is enough for me now.

32. Motorcycle Madness

When the plane arrived in New York in mid-December 1989, it was too late to get a bus home to Ithaca, so I slept outside in the cold, on a hill, rolled up in my sleeping bag. It would be my final night of roughing it. The next day I was home again in Ithaca. But I was now a changed man or, more accurately, a changing man. I was now in search of dignity more than anything else. I sought a sense of cleanliness. I had found a new way to live. I thought I could still oppose the industrial complex in America, but I didn't have to be a grungy, dirty hippie to prove my *bona fides*. I could be refined, more European. I felt as if Europeans knew how to enjoy life and lived with much more dignity than Americans. I wanted that, too. I no longer wanted to be an unwashed hippie. I wanted to be a clean, dignified person with my own views about organics, the earth, and education. This pivot toward refinement took freedom and travel to finally understand it. At times, my trip to Europe was full of despair; I had failed to plan well and bounced about from one city to the next. Yet my foolish rambling would pay dividends by broadening my mind . . . as I would find in the months ahead.

Now I planned to change, and my goal was to go to college, just like all the kids in Ithaca and my friend Lucía. I could do it, too. Why not? I didn't have to see myself as a burnout anymore. Yes, I smoked marijuana, but this didn't have to define me as some druggie burnout, as I had defined myself before going to Europe. I had dignity even as I was. Those drunk kids on the train in Denmark and the gentlemen in Amsterdam smoking hash had convinced me of this.

But first I needed to get my GED, the alternative to a high school diploma. So, I began to look into how to get that done. Being a tenth-grade dropout, I had much to learn.

Meanwhile, a few weeks after arriving from Europe, I went to dance and party at a bar called the Rongovian Embassy, which was about fifteen miles from home in a town called Trumansburg. It was a cold winter's night in early January 1990, following a snowstorm that stranded me in the house for days. My only vehicle was my motorcycle. The snow on the roads had been cleared, so while it would be a cold drive, it was doable. I was stir-crazy, so I went. There I met my friend Tom, who like me, also worked as an organic farmer.

The Rongo was a bar that catered to live alternative music. One of the best bands at that time was the Horseflies, a traditional American instrumental group of violin, oboes, guitars, and other wooden instruments all plugged into huge amps, electrifying the sound. They called their music polka dot hop electronic bug music (or some such thing). Their sound was an eclectic mix of old-world Americana, mixed with modern Rock-and-Roll and folk music. Once I asked a band member when he wrote a particular song I liked, and he looked at me as if I was an idiot, saying, "Dude, that song was written several hundred years ago."

Their music got so fast and wild that hundreds would erupt on the dance floor, jumping up and down so high and rhythmically that the entire wooden floor of the place would sway up and down as if it would completely collapse.

The Rongo was *the* place for all cool organic and wild hipsters of the time. The bar's architectural style has been called *nouveau rustique*. The few tables inside were all-natural wood—many had hand carvings on them. The forty-foot bar countertop, where beers from around the world were served, was made of a seamless slab of an enormous, old-growth, local tree.

I would go to the Rongo to completely let loose. A night of dancing there was more than any workout: it was like running full speed for several hours straight. Everyone would be dripping gallons of sweat during the sets of wild bug music. I danced free and uninhibited with hundreds of like-minded people.

That night in January, I had, of course, drunk many beers, but believed I had sweat out all the alcohol on the dancefloor (this theory is probably a wives' tale but seemed rational at the time). When the bar closed, as I was leaving, I noticed Tom and a young blond girl arm and arm, walking out. He noticed me mounting my bike as the snow was starting to fall lightly. He called over to me, "Hey man, do you need a ride?" Aware of the pretty girl with him I said, "No dude, I'll be fine; have fun." Tom later told me he was concerned about me but grateful I didn't ask him for a ride.

After bundling up, I jumped on my bike to start home. It was around 2 a.m. and well below freezing. I went down the road racing along at eighty miles per hour, full throttle, thinking the sooner I got home the sooner I would be warm (oh, the way a young mind works). It was a cloudless night. The way home was along Route 227, a rural road, empty that time of the evening. The waxing gibbous moon was beaming as bright as the sun. It held my attention. I had never seen such a beautiful moon. I dreamt for a moment. As I glared at that crystal moon, flying down the road, I hymned an ode deep in my heart.

Suddenly, I was flying through the air, seeing my motorcycle flying high as well, the light bouncing fifty feet into the air. We were both tumbling independently of one another. The moon had seduced me. I had not seen the turn in the road, barreling through it right onto the frozen ground. After bouncing and flying 150 horizontal feet, I landed in a ditch on the corner of Route 227 and Williamee Road. I could see the light of my bike shining into the sky like a beacon.

I laid there for what felt like only a few minutes but may have been an hour. I kept thinking I needed to get up but just wasn't ready. I was not in pain—just stunned and half conscious. Then a man appeared standing over me, asking me questions: "Are you ready to get up? Can I help you?" "Just give me a minute, I'm okay," I said. But he persisted, knowing I wasn't okay. Finally, he pulled me up and into his car. The bike's engine was still revving, but he couldn't find the keys, so we left it—the light still shining into the night sky. He asked, "Do you want to go to the hospital?" and I said, "No." The reason I said this was because I remembered my brother Russell's accident, how it led to a DUI, and I imagined the police were going to make me blow the breathalyzer if I went to the hospital. I didn't like or trust the police. So, he agreed to take me home, which was only about ten minutes away.

He dropped me off at my neighbor Preston's house since I was house-sitting for him and his wife while they were away on vacation. I was able to hobble inside. I took off my clothes and went into the lush waterbed, immediately falling asleep. I was only bleeding a small bit from several cuts, but there was no significant blood. I had been wearing a helmet.

When I woke up, the reality of the pain kicked in. I could not bend my left leg or put on my pants because of it. My knee was utterly immobile. I called Tom (who years later remembered the actual conversation):

"Oh, hey, sorry to bother you," I said.

"You not bothering me. I'm alone anyway. I dropped that girl off last night. What's up?" Tom replied.

"Can you get my bike?" I asked.

"You okay?" he asked.

"Broke my leg," I said.

"I'll come get you," he said.

"Can you get my bike first?" I asked.

Tom didn't listen to me. He came to get me first, and he drove me to the hospital, first passing by the wrecked motorcycle (later retrieving it for me). I noticed, as we stopped at the scene of the accident, that there was a telephone pole that I had barely missed ramming into. Had I hit that pole I would surely have been killed instantly.

Tom has an extraordinary memory. He remembers that when we entered the hospital, I made a pass at a cute nurse attending me, even while I was barely conscious, having passed out for a time from the pain. He told me later he admired me for my vigorous pursuit of women. This makes me blush, but he's probably right.

After some tests, the doctor determined I had broken a finger and a rib and sprained my ankle. But I needed to return for an MRI in a few days after the swelling receded in my immobile knee. Tom took me back to Preston's place.

Later that day, my brother Patrick came to see me, informing me that the police came to his house late the night before looking for me, since they had encountered the wrecked motorcycle (the bike's registration showing his home as my address). I felt that I had been lucky to have avoided a breathalyzer and DUI. Looking back now, the police were just doing their job, probably only looking for me out of concern for my wellbeing. But after all my past arrests, jail, juvy, and the confinement of Straight, I had no love for the police and wanted to stay away from them. Even today, at times, I feel disdain for them for no reason. I say "feel" since it's just an irrational leftover emotion from my days of running from police and authority.

After completing the MRI a few days later, the doctor told me that I had ripped the patellar tendon in my left knee and would require surgery. I checked into the hospital. I would be there for three days. They anesthetized me to operate, and I woke the next morning in the hospital bed with a leg cast.

My brother Patrick came to visit me the morning after my operation. He told me, "Dave, I have a letter from Germany for you here. It came in the mail today." It was from that mysterious girl Esther whom I had met near the Freiburg Minster in Germany. It was my first letter from her and a complete surprise. The message was sweet (somehow, I had made a good impression in my hippie state), yet serious, suggesting that I turn to God.

It was an ominous letter. I had already begun changing my life in order to find dignity, and I had been thinking about God, following the miracle that had happened to me in the Freiburg Minster. Now I was lying in a hospital bed, just a month after returning from Europe where my mind had expanded. And I was grateful to still be alive.

I wrote her back. We would begin a letter writing friendship.

33. Don Quixote de la Mancha

I started my extended period of recovery that winter. I could not walk for several months, so I was not working. Instead, I stayed home at my brother Patrick's house. Patrick was not there most days or nights, so I spent my time alone in a small living room in his large Victorian home, using the wood stove to keep warm. There was no television, and I didn't want one. Television for me was part of the industrial complex I wanted to avoid. So, with no other entertainment or distractions, I started to read continuously. I could do nothing else nor go anywhere.

When I was in Spain, I had heard about *Don Quixote of La Mancha* by Miguel de Cervantes, a famous book written at the turn of the seventeenth century. I had gotten a copy and read both volumes during my recovery. The fictional story follows the adventures of a Mr. Alonso Quixano, who is an avid reader of chivalric romance novels from medieval times. He reads so many of those books that he believes he is living in that time and loses all rationality. His reality becomes medieval, and he decides to set out to live chivalry, undoing wrongs and bringing justice to the world. He gives himself the name Don Quixote de la Mancha and seeks to be knighted, despite the practice having long been discontinued. He begins his journey on an old broken horse he believes to be a fresh steed, naming him Rocinante.

As he rides ("sallies") into the countryside, he is seeing the world, not as it is, but as he wants to see it. At one point, he sees what appears to him to be dragons (as often recounted in his chivalry books), though in reality are countryside windmills. He attacks them as dangerous fire-breathing wild beasts but ends up bloody and bruised himself, having crashed into actual spinning windmills.

He has many more misadventures based on the strange reality occurring in his mind. He often attempts to save others who do not need saving, and he courts a country wench who to him is a beautiful princess. He names her Dulcinea, and from then on she inspires all of his purity, honor, and nobility. He believes women should be treated with the utmost respect and refrains from illicit love. He loves God and practices his Catholic faith outwardly, honestly, and enthusiastically.

While the larger themes were profound, the book's humor was nonstop. I was barreling over in laughter (having to be careful, as sometimes laughter caused severe pain to my injuries). But that was part of its genius. It snuck into my mind deep and profound lessons through lunacy. I understood humor from early on. After all, I had been *Lou* growing up, short for lunatic, because of my silly streak. It was an affectionate moniker, but it stuck to me because it was at least, in part, correct.

Through genius humor, *Don Quixote* (or should I say Miguel de Cervantes) planted a fast-growing idea in the soil of my mind that had already been tilled and prepared in Europe. Something deep inside me would begin to change after reading this book; the idea would lead me to understand faith and virtue, would carry me to a new place in life, and would influence much of my philosophy for years to come.

As I read the classic tome, I began reflecting on all the past thoughts I had in light of what I was being presented with. My mind was making connections. The following, somewhat lengthy, is how I perceived the lessons in the book as applied to myself then and what I had begun thinking about.

Don Quixote was a man who had mental health problems. While his actions could be called insane, he was authentic. He had a pure love and genuine concern for others. He desired to do the will of God in honor and dignity, even though he was not apprehending reality correctly. Despite his incorrect perception of things, his motivations were real, pure, and kind. I began to wonder if this lesson could apply in my life—that is to say, to live virtue, faith, and honor in spite of not knowing if I perceived reality correctly.

After I began working with organics and before leaving for Europe, I had become an environmental hippie. All the friends I had were hippies; most were intellectual ones, not just unwashed druggies. They had profound ideas about how to order society through a return to nature. I found this philosophy attractive and bought into it. I began to defend Mother Earth through radical ecosabotage and began to believe that only nature and the natural rhythm of things had the answers to the big questions in life:

Where do I come from? The earth.

What is my role? To preserve the earth.

How should I live? Organically.

I did not believe in the ideas my father tried to instill in me as a child: that I was a soul created to live with God in heaven and to get there I must live a religious and virtuous life. My mother-earth philosophy had replaced this. Because of this, I had become a sort of nihilist when it came to traditional societal norms and social structures. I did not believe in things like marriage or institutions like organized religion; I saw them all as products of industrialization and the commercialization of natural man. Somehow, over thousands of years, the industrialists had won the argument, even though the natural state of man was superior.

Yes, I now saw religion in a better light since Europe, but I still wondered what good was it really? All men and women need is love for the earth and to live by nature. We didn't need to overcome nature with fancy homes, air conditioners, and over-development. There was this struggle in my mind: was human existence on earth nothing but earth, sky, life, and death? Or was there this need for God, virtue, and something beyond?

Sustainability and the natural cycle of life seemed to answer most questions, not the fluff of religion. I thought all these ideas of religion might be just constructs of man, figments of the imagination or paternalistic control. They were Marx's *opiate of the people*: a way to escape from what is real, in hopes for the next life in paradise.

Before going to Europe, I didn't see any point to such virtues of faith, dignity, and respect for others. I didn't know what they were for, if all was just wild nature. But in Europe, I began to see love, respect, faith, and dignity, and I grew attracted to them. Even Gómara's book on Cortés pointed to this: the Europeans wanted the Aztecs to understand that human sacrifice was evil, going against dignity and the right to life.

The idea of dignity I discovered in Europe was a small step toward my understanding the truth of man, but one that didn't necessarily require religion since I had no idea how anyone could proclaim a universal doctrine of man. It seemed as if there was some great veil between man and the truth of all things. There seemed to be no way to peek beyond the veil, to discover the absolute way of truth. If it was not the hippies with their pure nature theory, then who was it? Was it the Catholics, Bible-believing Christians, or Buddhists? They were all so different—all had different social constructs and teachings. It seemed impossible to know for sure.

But oddly, *Don Quixote* would help me reach a compromise. I could not know the certain truth of how to live the absolute best way, or of who was correct in organizing society and man. But as Don Quixote had done, I could choose to live under one set of rules and ideas, even if I perceived reality erroneously. I could not know what was behind the veil of reality and truth with absolute certainty, but I could make my best estimation of how it might be.

Perhaps, I could never come to finally find the absolute truth about the origins, nature, and final goal of man. It seemed it would be impossible to find such certainty. No one on the planet had, I imagined. Yet I could still choose to perform certain virtues that some religions practiced: honor, respect, love, and faith, for example. And I could even, perhaps, participate in some institutions that appeared to be helpful for living a complete life, even if I did not know if they were indeed the way man was meant to live.

I was not ready to embrace this ideal, but a little seedling of it was conceived in my mind during my reading of *Don Quixote*. Writing this now, I can almost see a pattern of God as a gardener: allowing the land to fallow for a time, tilling the soil, planting some seeds in fall and others in spring, sending water in due time, and eventually reaping the harvest. It was as if the Roanoke Cemetery had proven to me the existence of the Creator of nature; Gómara's *Conquest of Mexico* had convinced me of an objective moral and natural law; and Cervantes' *Don Quixote* had then taken me to the next step, which was to teach me subjectively (or emotionally) which specific path I could follow in order to learn more about the natural and moral law and, perhaps, God himself. But I am getting ahead of myself.

34. Bob Dylan & the Bible

Having read Gómara's *Conquest of Mexico* and now Cervantes' *Don Quixote*, I began to see a recurring sourcebook used over and over again: it was quotations of and references to the Bible. I had thought of the Bible as a collection of teachings on Judaism and Christianity, as my father had tried to teach me. I had never seen it as a literary source until now. My mother loved books and encouraged me to write, but she never spoke of the Bible as being of any interest.

As I sat alone all winter, my leg immobile, I continued reading yet still always listening to music. I started to hear references to the Bible while listening to my favorite musician, Bob Dylan. As I was becoming more aware of history, art, and religion, I began to understand while listening to him that his biblical references were not infrequent. For example, in the song *Sweetheart Like You,* he speaks of the father's house having *many mansions,* which I felt had something to do with the Bible. I would later find out it is a direct quote from the Gospel of John (14:2).

These sources, Bob Dylan, *Don Quixote,* and *The Conquest of Mexico,* all sparked my interest to want to read the Bible, not so much for theology as my father had done, but for literary and historical use. The Bible seemed to be the penultimate source of all great literature and art. Why was that? I wondered.

One Dylan album that particularly piqued my curiosity was entitled, *Infidels.* I could relate to the title since I thought myself an infidel, someone who rejected the religion of my youth. And supposedly, this was Dylan's first post-Christian album, released in 1983 after he had allegedly rejected his earlier conversion to Christianity. The entire album was captivating to me. I thought, why does the internal album artwork show him kneeling in the dirt on the Mount of Olives, overlooking the current Temple Mount in Jerusalem? I did not know what any of this was at the time, but the images and lyrics inflamed my heart.

One of the album's tracks entitled *Man of Peace* seemed to refer to a sly and tricky satanic figure who fools mankind, coming as a man of peace to the planet. Who is this man—some antichrist? But the first track on the album, entitled *Jokerman,* took hold of me. It was a profound puzzle that I wished to understand. It seemed to be about a divine mythical person, who would not reveal himself in full to any one group of people in history but instead was someone who straddled all of it, showing himself in small pieces and sometimes contradictory forms over all recorded time.

Who is this Jokerman? The very first line of the song seemed to refer to Moses having parted the Red Sea and providing manna for the Jews in the desert. In another line, Dylan appears to refer to Moses having made a bronze snake. Another line appears to refer to Jesus having been a friend of Mary Magdalene, preventing her from being stoned, and another relates to the parable of the damned rich man, calling out to Abraham. I had vaguely remembered these references from my early Bible studies at home.

Yet Dylan kept referring to this man, whoever he was, as a Jokerman, hiding himself, allowing himself to be seen only in pieces, while dancing and reveling at the moon. Throughout history, God was shedding layers of himself each time a new religion came along. There seemed to be kernels of truth in all major religions, but coming to the full truth seemed impossible. It was as if God was playing as a Joker, never wanting to be fully known to men.

Was this true? Was God unknowable? What was behind this veil of obscurity? I had never been able to see beyond it. Could I find what was true?

If I could not find the truth, I thought, could I at least find a way to feel content and happy in life not knowing? This was the lesson I had taken by reading *Don Quixote*. Was it necessary to know the complete truth in its totality before I could agree to live by certain adopted cultural norms?

So, with all that time on my hands, handicapped and holed up all winter, with all these references and imaginings in my mind, I started to read the Bible. I wanted to know if I could divine God from this ultimate source or at least better educate myself to understand history, literature, and art. I started at page one of the book of Genesis and began to read, even if I did not comprehend much of what I was reading. I read it slowly while continuing to read other things.

It would take me a year to read the entire Bible. Much of it was boring, like the legal prescriptions in Deuteronomy, but many of the stories were quite fascinating. When I read the book of Job, I felt as if I understood that suffering man, not literally, but I understood how he felt. His friends believed he was cursing God, yet God knew he was not. He was entirely and incomparably incapacitated and yet kept his conscience clear. I was not like him in keeping the faith, but I appreciated how no one believed in him, yet he knew himself and would not bend to anyone. I thought of myself in this way after my time in Straight. No peer pressure could turn my will. I was all in when I believed in something, no matter what pain came to me. Society could never convince me of something I would not be convinced of on my own—just as Straight was unable to break my wild heart.

I was also enchanted and aroused by the Song of Songs, a biblical book about a man speaking of, among other things, his beloved's beautiful, warm breasts. Such artistic and sensual language was not something I had ever known was in the Bible. Apparently, my father had skipped over that book when we sat around our dinner table as children reading passages.

After that long, spiritual winter, while reading the Bible and *Don Quixote*, I couldn't help but start to question whether the God of the Bible had more significant legitimacy than my mother-nature approach to life, as its ancient stories impressed my mind.

Spring soon came, my leg was healing, and I was getting out of the house. My metaphysical winter was solitary and remarkable; I felt like Rip Van Winkle having woken up with a mind full of new ideas. Yet it did not change my lifestyle dramatically. My love of and need for sex still trumped my newly spiritual underpinnings. My natural earth ideas still provided me with cover and rationale. Yet many seeds had been planted in my mind over these past few months.

The one change I knew I had wanted and was fully effectuating was that of gaining dignity. I didn't want to let that idea go; it didn't require me to change morally in any way, but it helped me clean up my life. My clothes were now cleaner, my beard was trimmed, and I was using deodorant again. I found a self-study program to obtain my GED and had begun to study. I felt accomplished since I had finished several large-volume classic books as well as much of the Old Testament. I was proud of myself.

35. Dalai Lama & the Universe

Since moving to Ithaca, I had many deep conversations with friends and acquaintances. Ithacans loved to talk deeply; they were not superficial people. Any conversation I had with others about the truth of mankind, the earth, and nature always seemed to include the first and most important principle of being *open to the universe,* an idea I now believe can be traced to the then famous Cornell professor, Carl Sagan. Being open to the universe meant to not dogmatically oppose any idea but rather to be open to all ideas, whether it be scientific atheism or religion—to be respectful, to coexist. It seemed to be rooted in the idea that there was no one primary truth; instead, truth was a concept that various ages and races defined differently. No one can judge another since moral truth was relative.

In Ithaca, there were many gradations of alternative thought: there were the unwashed hippies, who for example loved the Grateful Dead and experimented with drugs; then there were the intellectuals like my neighbor Preston, who believed in Marxism and population control; there were people like Aron, who tried to live consistent with the natural earth in all things, including childbirth and conception; and then there were those taking their thought to a higher level, practicing eastern spirituality. Regarding the final category, it is not to say that all were formally practicing spirituality—some would emulate it through mediums of yoga—but others would, in fact, entirely convert to Buddhism or other eastern spiritualties and religions.

The spiritual head of one form of Buddhism, the Dalai Lama, was then and is to this day revered in Ithaca. When I lived there, his U.S. headquarters was a house located downtown where several of his monks lived. By 1991, this house would become known as the Namgyal Monastery and Institute of Buddhist Studies.

The Dalai Lama is considered the reincarnated successor of Avalokiteśvara, the Bodhisattva of Compassion. From the year 1642, there have been fourteen reincarnations of the Dalai Lama. Each one has headed the Tibetan government in Lhasa. In 1959, the Chinese invaded and took over Tibet, causing the Dalai Lama to go into exile. The Dalai Lama fled to India, moving his primary residence and monastery in exile to Dharamsala. Later, the Monastery in Ithaca was opened as its North American seat. Monks from

Dharamsala were then (and still are today) rotated in and out of the Ithaca branch. Typically, there were about five in residence there in Ithaca.

Frequently, I would walk by their bright red house, located on Aurora Street. On the porch, there were always dozens of Tibetan prayer flags flying in the wind. I would go up to the house to get a copy of the *Snow Lion* (then the only Tibetan publication in America) and would read the public postings about upcoming events. There were plenty of prayer and meditation activities year around. Once I attended an event held by the monks at Cornell University: the creation of a Mandala, a work of art made with only colored sand. It took the monks several days to create it. It was tranquil watching the holy and peaceful monks generate the sand artwork with small tube-funnel sticks called *chak-pur* that make a buzzing yet spiritual sound. The Mandala has a symbolic purpose: it supposedly helps a person to reach deeper levels of the subconscious mind.

After the Mandala had been viewed for a few days, the monks gathered up the sand into jars and poured it all into the Ithaca River as a spiritual oblation to the town. This finale was supposed to symbolize the transitory nature of material life and the world itself. This was curious for me. I, too, wanted to explore my subconscious mind as deeply as possible, and I fully understood the offering of art to nature in this way.

The Dalai Lama himself came to Ithaca often, and one year when I was there, he came to speak at Cornell. Dressed in his flowing bright scarlet robes, he greeted us, a large crowd of people that came to admire and listen to him. We all loved his radiant persona and message of peace. No, I was not ready to follow pure Tibetan Buddhism, nor were many in the audience, but we all loved the ideas of expanding one's unconscious self and attunement to nature. His voice and presentation were peaceful. He seemed a humble man. I thought him a truly good man, though not divine.

The full array of people representing Ithaca's alternative community were there, including the liberals, hippies, transients, astrologists, therapists, crystal and light healers. They all admired him and desired to expand their minds. The Dalai Lama and Tibetan Buddhism provided us with a feeling that we were open to all great religions and spiritualities; while none had universal truth, all had value.

I wanted to be open to all forms of religion and spirituality. What I understood about the Dalai Lama's form of Buddhism, as interpreted by my friends, reminded me of Kahlil Gibran's *The Prophet* that I had read as a child, which alluded to this fundamental unity of all religions.

But I was quickly learning that, while my friends all spoke of being open to all forms of belief—agnosticism, Buddhism, Hinduism, Islam, and even some forms of Christianity—they would not be open to Catholicism. I was in no way defending Catholicism, but I found it odd that all of my friends seemed united in opposing just this one religion. Having learned much over the past year about Catholicism, having read *Don Quixote* and the *Conquest of Mexico,* and from my ramblings in Europe, I thought that, at the very least, this ancient church should get the same respect as the others. I thought it likely the Dalai Lama would agree, though I had no proof of this. He seemed open, honest, and friendly.

But I began to understand why there was this irrational revulsion toward it. My friends believed the Catholic Church was the primary cause of pain and guilt in the world, due to its close-mindedness on sexuality—the fundamental problem being its stance on contraception. I agreed to some extent. Prohibiting contraception led to an overpopulated world for one, I thought. And secondly, why should I allow a church to tell me about how I should engage in my sexuality—a purely natural function?

But this revulsion to Catholicism felt like hatred to me—something that one rarely sees in an alternative spiritual seeker, as so many thought of themselves in Ithaca. I did not agree with Catholicism's views on sex but, to be consistent, I thought we should at least be open to it in the same way we were open to all religions and ideas.

36. Coitus Interruptus

Everyone seemed to know about the Catholic Church's prohibition of contraception. Contraception was continually on my mind, too. I had started dating a Jewish girl, Martha, who had some of the European beauty and dignity I liked. She had long, thick, and curly black hair, black eyes, dark skin, and a Mediterranean look—a true *la belle juive*. She was more educated than I was, but we were both very alternative minded. In one area though, she was much more progressive than me: she did not believe in monogamy. She thought it an outdated social construct. She liked dating me, but she was living with another young man. Yet she was not a liar or a cheat; she was open to me about her polyamory (and supposedly was open to the other man, whom I never met). I accepted it. I liked to think I accepted her because I was open to all ideas, but, in reality, it was because her coquettish beauty fed my desires. In actuality, I felt jealous. I didn't understand why I felt this, however, since my natural-based nihilism did not have room for the institution of monogamy; this was a concept of industrialization, I thought.

My mind was in knots after Europe and my spiritual winter: Was I just a part of nature, or was there some greater concept? Was God knowable? Was the God of the Old Testament the true God? Was there a proper way to live? So many questions. I was confused; my theories were all becoming uncertain. I went along with Martha because she was attractive, and I needed her. I needed sex.

In the practice of sex, however, there is this little side effect called pregnancy. This was especially true among alternatives like myself, who opposed the use of chemicals whenever possible, both in our food and in our bodies. Many alternative women opposed the pill pursuant to this view.

Yet, sex was an absolute. It was a necessary part of living, I thought. In fact, it was more than just part of nature and necessity; it was a way to obtain spiritual experiences. Having sex was like being transported out of time and space, even if for only a short time, and it was all natural.

So then, how to avoid this dilemma? Pregnancy was something no one wanted, except for a few committed couples. There were several methods to prevent it, though none ideal. There was the condom. Yet for me, the idea of having to purchase a commercial product on the market seemed to interfere with the true concept of nature. Nature should not require the purchasing of products. Moreover, it affected the spiritualness of the act—at least for the man, I thought.

Then there was vasectomy for men and tubal ligation for women. My neighbor Preston had undergone a vasectomy. He wanted to live according to nature as close as possible, in cutting wood for his fire, recycling, reusing waste, growing his own food, and even in sex. But for him, a vasectomy was required to prevent the world overpopulation crisis. Moreover, it was not entirely unnatural as a doctor merely tied off his tubes, which he believed could be reversed later. But to me, it seemed illogical to cut a natural function of the body, like cutting off the tongue so as not to taste.

Then there was the diaphragm. This seemed to be the primary form of contraception for alternatives. Yet many women did not want to allow this into their bodies, as Martha did not.

So, there was a constant battle, not only in my mind but in my sexual practices. Martha and I wanted to avoid pregnancy since we were not ready for a family, but we were against chemicals and artificial plastic objects interfering with our natural function. And I did not want a vasectomy, nor did Martha want a tubal ligation. Yet sex was an absolute.

There was only one choice: *coitus interruptus*. This was not ideal; however, it was a compromise for me. Even this posed a problem in my natural earth logic:

Do the animals withdraw? No.

If not, then why should man? Well, to prevent pregnancy.

But why should man want to prevent pregnancy if it is the natural result of sex? Because then I will have to raise the child.

But animals raise their young, so why shouldn't I? There is no answer other than because I want the pleasure of sex but not the natural outcome of it.

Only my friend Aron seemed to have the logical and proper response. His take (it seemed to me) was that sex requires monogamy for the purposes of child rearing. He refused chemicals and artificial objects not only in his food but in sex as well. To have a happy and healthy sex life, one must commit to just one so that if babies result, the couple can care for them and raise them. This idea seemed the most natural. If not, then pursuant to nature, why shouldn't parents freely abandon their children after a year or two when the child can scrounge for food, and we would all then live in a pure state of nature without culture, education, art, and society.

It was this endless series of questions that inflicted my mind, seeming to lead to the conclusion that men and women are meaningfully different than animals. There appeared to be something beyond pure nature that drove and regulated mankind. If organic nature did not provide the answers, where could I learn them? Once again, I ran into this veil of hidden knowledge and understanding. Why couldn't mankind know the answers to these questions? Why is there this veil clouding reality anyway? Why can't we just know the truth and act accordingly? Perhaps God is a Jokerman.

Using my reason, I had to admit that Aron seemed to be right. But, of course, a solution for mankind cannot be based on just the idea of one man. Instead, there was already an ancient remedy to this problem: marriage. And it was notably the Catholic Church that seemed to be the closest to these ideas: the role of sex naturally leads to procreation and, therefore, should occur within the stability of two parents willing to raise a child fully to adulthood, educating him or her, providing culture, and passing on this same social norm to them. I thought, could it be true that men and women require monogamy and marriage for the proper rearing of children?

The whole problem of procreation and marriage created confusion in my mind. This uncertainty created a ticking time bomb in my theory that organic nature could answer all questions of mankind. The more I had sex, the more my thoughts about the uniqueness of man and procreation bothered me. My conscience began to rebel against my body's needs, but *coitus interruptus* provided a satisfactory compromise, for now.

While Martha and I continued with our strained (and jealous) polyamorous relationship, I started to spend some time with another woman whom I liked, a motorcycle adventurer like myself, but who was married and had children. One day, in a moment of *Dionysian surrender*, we secretly had sex together. This triggered an enormous guilt inside of me. I felt as if I betrayed her husband and children. I tried to rationalize this away using my organic theories of life: that animals don't regard marriage and family and can have sex with any partner. But this approach no longer worked. All of my philosophical seeking had caused me mental anguish. My conscience was tangled. I wished I had been closed to all this new philosophy and literature twisting my mind. *Don Quixote,* the *Conquest of Mexico,* my openness to all ideas and religions, my desire for dignity, the miracle in Germany, and my current reading of the Old Testament—all of this was deconstructing my theories of pure nature.

The God I was reading about in the Bible, as well as a natural God that seemed to require monogamy, began hounding me. My conscience began to burn, like the fifty-foot fires of the Santa Cruz hippie camp. I was forced to be open to this greater-than-mother-nature God. I knew I had to try to understand the ways of this God if I wanted peace.

37. My Cottage Home

By early summer of 1990, I was walking with the help of a cane I had crafted out of a tree limb, having been able to drop my aluminum crutches sometime before. Because I could work again, my neighbor Preston offered me a small cottage on his property to live in, in exchange for work, and I accepted. It was just a five-minute walk from my brother Patrick's place, so I could continue to help him when he needed. But I wanted independence.

Patrick and I were both going through many changes. He pulled me aside before I left, wanting to tell me something serious. He told me that I was going to be the first one in our family to know. He said, "I am coming out. I have always had an attraction to men." He was now willing to tell everyone he was gay. He said, "I can no longer ignore these feelings or pretend not to have them."

Both of us were similarly sensitive souls: we both wrote poems, we both liked to sing and play music, both liked art, beauty, and alternative living, and I think both of us were less masculine than our peers. Neither of us fit a typical American manly stereotype. Yet I had never seen him be affectionate with a man before. In fact, I had known several of his girlfriends. He never had a problem getting girlfriends. He would often have a girlfriend as well as several women as friends. He related easily to women, and they to him. He could speak their language. It was hard for me to meet women, but Patrick was a natural. In fact, I wished I had his gift of attracting and befriending women. He had a confidence and naturalness that I just lacked.

I was not judgmental about his announcement, but I thought it strange because of his success with women. I just accepted it. But in the privacy of my own mind, I thought about it in the light of my current philosophical confusion about heterosexual sex. Regarding pure nature, it seemed unnatural to me (though others would argue that in nature there exists some homosexual activity). Regarding contraception, it did not apply since there could be no conception. But if there could be no conception, then for what purpose was it? In what other area of life is pleasure a means in and of itself, I thought. Perhaps eating? But no, because we must eat for nutrition. But, in fact, I too was enjoying the purely physical aspect of sex without its natural outcome. So, it was not something that concerned me deeply as I had more pressing things on my mind. It was his life, and he was free to choose whatever way he wanted.

I would continue to see him often, but for now, I was ready for my new solo home. My cottage was about thirty feet long and fifteen feet wide. It was made of cement and wood. My living area was about twenty by fifteen, and the other ten feet was for storing tools and my motorcycle. My motorcycle still ran after I had fixed it up. I used it to get around. In fact, it was better than riding in a car since my busted leg could not bend to get in and out of a vehicle nor could it push a clutch hard enough, but I could comfortably sit up straight on the motorcycle and manipulate its pedals. In fact, I would take it to my doctor visits and the store when needed. It was quickly identifiable as having been in a crash, but it ran, and it was all I had. I would attach my cane to the back and go where I needed to go.

In the cottage, I had no bathroom, but I had a large bucket with a lid. I would take it in and out of the home, and every few days I would dig a deep hole in the property and bury the waste. I had ample, five-gallon tanks of water I used in a sink without plumbing. I would take showers inside Preston's house, which was just across the property. The cottage had several windows but no south facing one to allow in the sun. Thus, it was often cold inside, but I had a wood stove that worked very well as the house was insulated. I had some rudimentary seating, a kitchenette with a hotplate and mini fridge, and a futon thrown on the floor for sleeping. I had no television, but I did have a good stereo system to play all my music. I had my guitar, a couple of books, the *Snow Lion* and *Earth First!* journals lying around, my Bible, and a few posters on the wall from my trip to Europe.

In exchange for living there, I milked Preston's cow every morning (squirting the teat straight into my coffee cup as well), fetched the eggs from the chickens, cut cords of wood from his forest for both his and my woodstoves, put a new roof on my cottage, and helped him around his house sheet-rocking and painting, among other things. I was even called upon to chop off the rooster's head and pluck out its feathers so that we could eat it. Catching the rooster with his sharp-pronged spurs was a difficult task, but I finally did it. I was to live there for the next year, working with Preston and enjoying the farm life.

One summer I attended the Rainbow Gathering in the Finger Lakes National Forest, just a few minutes from my home. The first Rainbow Gathering was held in 1972 as an outgrowth of the 1969 Woodstock music festival. Since then, these gatherings have been held annually in different public forests around the country (and still are today). That summer near my home, thousands came from all over to camp out in the woods for a week. It was a Brigadoon-type village of like-minded alternative types—hippies seeking peace, life, and light. Everyone was dancing, praying, and meditating in a group spirit of love and unity. At least that was the idea. There was no commercialization, and all was bartered—food, clothing, and, of course, drugs. I came for the apex finale, where all joined in a massive drum circle, praying for a moment of peace in the world.

But I camped only one night since I experienced a problematic transcendent dream that was so real it scared me away. I dreamt of being lifted high into the air swiftly but smoothly as if propelled upward by balloons. Then, for a moment, I was floating on a great hand, which held me in total peace above the entire camp, overlooking all from a thousand feet. Suddenly, the great hand upon which I floated dropped me, and I fell to the earth rapidly and dramatically. I knew that once I hit the ground, I would surely die. But right before impact, I woke; my heart was racing, and I was in a deep sweat.

I had never had a dream like that. I attributed it to a foul energy in the community. This light healing gathering did not feel natural or positive to me. It felt as if evil-personified was alive there. Many of the attendees were taking mind-altering drugs like LSD and magic mushrooms. I had not taken LSD since leaving California years earlier. In fact, the Rainbow Gathering reminded me of the camp in Santa Cruz but on a much larger scale. I had grown away from this and had a bad taste for it now. The disappearance of Angel from the Santa Cruz camp had left my heart distressed. I had matured since then and was now on a different spiritual path, one that included the God I was learning about in my readings and imaginings. This dream was a warning from him to stay away from this, to stay away from evil, I thought.

38. Jesus the Radical

As the summer ended and the fall of 1990 began, I was finally reaching the end of my reading of the Old Testament, and I started to believe in the God presented in its ancient pages. I was not changing my life dramatically, but I had lost boundless faith in my mother-earth nature theories.

I then started on page one of the New Testament books. Martha and I were still together, but I was receiving more frequent letters from my German Christian friend, Esther.

Suddenly, the Bible started to shake me. No longer was it just an intellectual exercise in understanding literary sources and coming to appreciate the Jewish God. The Old Testament finished, the Bible was now turning into a *force majeure*. Jesus suddenly splashed across the pages. He jumped out at me.

He appeared to love nature and the outdoors as I, walking and camping all over the countryside. And he was a radical, I thought. I had been a radical environmentalist, opposed to a commercialized and industrialized world. Now I was discovering Jesus, smashing the tables of the money changers in the temple, exclaiming that they were commercializing the sacred place. Only a radical would do such a thing, overturning the apple cart, where everyone else would just accept and go along with it all.

Jesus was also claiming to fulfill the Old Testament I had just read. He was kind and gentle with women, even prostitutes and sinners. And he was slamming the overly pious Jews of his time:

> Woe to you, scribes and Pharisees, hypocrites! For you tithe mint, dill, and cummin, and have neglected the weightier matters of the law: justice and mercy and faith. It is these you ought to have practiced without neglecting the others. You blind guides! You strain out a gnat but swallow a camel! . . . For you clean the outside of the cup and of the plate, but inside they are full of greed and self-indulgence" (Matthew 23:23–25).

I hated piosity and hypocrisy, having seen it before: as a little boy, when my father took me to church in South Lyon, I remembered seeing men in the pews, who I would see later looking at Playboy magazines in the markets around town. And growing up it seemed all religious people were more concerned with properness in societal norms than truth or justice.

I was shocked by Jesus, taken back that I would be impressed by this man, who I had seen only as a symbol of sentimentality and weakness. I thought of him as I thought of my father, someone who rejected risk and the grandeur of the world, someone judgmental and self-righteous and overly virtuous. I thought my father wanted to hide from the world in a bubble of nice religion. He liked to stay home, and I wanted to see the world. I was a risk taker who derided safety. I was worldly, and he would speak of contempt for the world. This is how I characterized all Christians. Yet, here was a Jesus I never knew, telling his followers to be "shrewd as serpents" (Matthew 10:16). I had always thought of Jesus as this meek and humble man and of Christianity as all about saying no to everything that was fun or exciting. Here instead was a natural but radical man, breaking the conventions of his own time, including piousness and commercialization. I was shockingly impressed.

As I spun through its pages, I did not change my life immediately. I started to appreciate my burgeoning understanding of Judaism, Jesus, the Bible, and the history of Christianity. But my thoughts of turning toward Jesus as the Son of God began to grow exponentially.

I think that if I had read the New Testament without the past years of experiences and learning, it would have meant little to me. But God had seemingly been tilling the soil of my heart. Now, everything was leading to God: my theories of nature pointed to him, my experiences in Europe spoke of him, and even my love of art and music was now infected by him. And this him, who I began to see as a daring and dynamic man, was claiming divinity.

As soon as I read the New Testament, my mind and heart went into hyperdrive. I thought that this man Jesus, who claims to sit at the right hand of God, may be able to break through that Jokerman veil of obscurity and help me to find the truth about how mankind is to live.

39. The Gulf War & Armageddon

Around this time a conflagration in the Middle East had begun, when Saddam Hussein invaded and annexed Kuwait. President George H. W. Bush was preparing an all-out assault to free Kuwait. There was talk everywhere of the end of days. Israel and the Holy Land were threatened. Baghdad had been called the cradle of civilization, where many believed the biblical Garden of Eden had once existed. I remembered my father telling me as a child that the end of the world would start as a conflagration in the Middle East. It seemed to be coming true. The events spoken of were as a great Armageddon coming; secular newspapers and magazines were even speaking in these terms.

One day I was working in my neighbor Preston's field, thrashing a scythe, hacking down long-growth grass, when Army recruiters had come to visit me. Preston told them where to find me. The two men dressed in uniform came up to me smiling. I met them while still carrying the giant, sharp-edged scythe in my hands. I still had much bitterness in me toward the industrialized world, and this included the entire military complex. I was a man of peace from as early as I can remember, even having a peace sign tattoo. I hated war, fighting, and anything to do with bombs and the like. At that moment, I hated these two men as well, for they represented a world I opposed. I told them, "I am not interested in joining the army. I believe in peace, not war." But they were not satisfied. So, then I told them, "I am handicapped due to a motorcycle accident," showing them the large scar on my knee. They had heard enough and said, "Well, then you can't join," and departed. I was relieved. I had no desire to fight in the Middle East, taking part in destroying the center of civilization without knowing what it was all really about.[21]

Soon, as I was finishing the New Testament by beginning the final book of Revelation, my entire life seemed to be crashing in on me. I had slowly begun to believe in Jesus (wondering that perhaps he was the true Son of God), though it was still in a philosophical, not practical, way. At the same time, I conversely began to fear the devil as well. Jesus did not shy away from speaking of him as a real spiritual being. And in Revelation, he is a great dragon that has been seized and sealed off from the world for a thousand years (Revelation 20:2). But perhaps now his time had come to lay waste to the earth, I thought.

I couldn't help but fear that maybe this great apocalypse in Revelation was coming true, that the world was ending and the terror of Satan had begun.

My fear of the devil was getting stronger. I always knew of him. My young seven-year-old mind first became aware of him after seeing the film *The Exorcist*. I would then experience him again among friends who followed him through music, in brooms and broken glass in the Roanoke graveyard, in bestiality in the bars of Juárez, in the dark nature nymphs among the fires of the Santa Cruz hippie camp, and in the disturbing dream at the Rainbow Gathering.

As I was getting closer to God and Jesus in my reading, I felt as if the devil was trying to close in on me, in the corridors of the night, watching my weaknesses. I remembered the lovely, caring, and beautiful women of Europe—so filled with dignity, including, of course, Lucía and Esther. But my desire for sex with women was my primary problem in choosing to follow God. Women filled my mind constantly. Now I had Martha for love and sex, but my mind was torn with new, beautiful, pure memories and ideas. I was obsessed over women. But as I spent time reading the Scriptures with a spirit of appreciation for Jesus, I began to feel this obsession with women being expelled by a growing love for God (as devils being expelled into swine, Matthew 8:28–32).

While I read Revelation and saw the bombs flying in the Middle East, I was worried about my own soul and the world itself. I could see the parallels between the Gulf War and what I now began to believe. While we (the U.S.) were about to win the war, I had not yet won my own personal battle of accepting Jesus and becoming a Christian. I was still at war with myself.

40. The Vine Dresser

The war came to an end on February 28, 1991, my twenty-second birthday. And at this same time, I began to feel the war in my heart had started to end. That spring I began to feel like a blossoming flower, opening with color and gentleness. It seemed the fear of the end times had passed, and I felt as if I wanted to continue this blooming of my mind to God. I had more and more come to believe that Jesus was divine. I knew I would have to come to grips with how I was to live if I were to accept him fully.

I began to keep a journal about my budding spirituality. I wrote:

> *Dear God and great forces that move my mind,*
> *Thank you for allowing me some happiness and contentment.*
> *You who ever mystifies me.*
> *More and more, I have no questions left.*
> *More and more, I have more answers than I can use.*
> *Less and less, do I understand anything on earth.*
> *More and more, I feel I haven't a right for questions, especially when I know they will never be answered on earth.*
> *They linger in my mind now, but for the life of me, I cannot comprehend them.*
> *All that I can understand is that I love you, in my way, right or wrong.*

During this time I started working full-time as a vine dresser at Lakewood Farms, a vineyard located in Watkins Glen, about fifteen miles from Reynoldsville in an area called the Finger Lakes region, well known for its winemaking. A vine dresser essentially prepares the vines for spring, cutting and pruning for optimal growth. The old vine trunks are large and gnarly, hibernating in winter, but in spring they begin to grow new vine offshoots. My job was to prepare their growth by trimming and tying the vines to the wire, so that when the new branches began to grow and produce grapes, the wires would support their weight.

I would start early in the morning before the sun rose from the eastern end of the lake. The big purple sky was usually overcast, and cold moisture steadily filled the air, freezing my hands as I walked up and down the sloping acres of vines. It was a solitary job. I was by myself the entire eight-hour days with just my thoughts, the weather, the pruner tool, twist ties, and the endless vines. My mind was now full of passages I had read in the Scriptures (just as Don Quixote's mind was full of readings of his chivalry books). I couldn't help but remember those about vine growing. At one point I would read Jesus say:

> I am the true vine, and my Father is the vinegrower. He removes every branch in me that bears no fruit. Every branch that bears fruit he prunes to make it bear more fruit. . . . Abide in me as I abide in you. . . . Whoever does not abide in me is thrown away like a branch and withers; such branches are gathered, thrown into the fire, and burned (John 15:1–6).

I was happy, but these passages struck fear in me as I tied-off vines all day long. I was not yet a full follower of Jesus. All of my life had been lived without believing in Jesus. I had opposed him and was now feeling alone and regretful. I began to fear being thrown away and burned if I didn't fully accept him, just as the paintings had shown in the Del Prado in Madrid. I didn't want to be dragged into the fiery pit of hell.

As I worked in the fields, I was speaking directly to Jesus and often yelling at him. I was at peace usually but in turmoil as well. I was becoming a believer in Jesus by fire and love; he was inescapable.

I was still not speaking to anyone about my thoughts; I was the same person outwardly, but inwardly Jesus was invading my mind. I felt happiness and joy in spring, yet I also felt despair as I regretted my past. Could I gain control over my present and rout out these feelings of pain?

41. Jesus: Our Destiny

I had been studying all winter to obtain my high school diploma equivalency, and finally, the test date came that spring. I took the test in Watkins Glen and passed! It was a proud moment in my life to have finally earned my GED after having quit school in the tenth grade. I was still pursuing the idea that I could live an educated life with the dignity I had seen in Europe.

Now I could go to college. I quickly applied to the City University of New York, Brooklyn College of Journalism. I wanted to be an international photojournalist, traveling the world reporting on events. It fit my desire to see the world. I would have to wait a few months for the answer to come.

At this same time, I finished reading Revelation. It had been a year since I had started reading the first page of Genesis, and now I had completed the entire Bible.

I soon received a small package from Germany—it was from Esther. It had been over a year since I met her in Freiburg, and since then we wrote several letters back and forth. I had come to learn that she was a nondenominational Christian, believing all of God's revelation is contained only in the Bible. She believed that one need only give one's life to Jesus and would then be saved and go to heaven. Nothing else was required for salvation.

In this package was something more than just a letter, it was a book entitled *Jesus: Our Destiny,* originally written in German by Wilhelm Busch and later translated into English and many other languages. Wilhelm Busch had been a German youth pastor and evangelist during the Nazi period in Germany. The Third Reich had attempted to Nazify the German Protestant church, which Busch firmly and openly opposed. This led to his arrest and lengthy incarceration. Upon release, he would go back to preaching the gospel, and eventually, an SS commissioner ordered him to be expelled from the territory of Hessen, where he lived and worked. He refused and was retaken to prison. After the war he continued as a youth pastor, adopting his main thematic slogan *Jesus our destiny*, which he would keep using until his death in 1966.

The book I now held in my hands, which according to the forward had sold millions of copies worldwide, was compiled from a series of radio addresses he had given. His overall thematic proposition was that of the centrality of Jesus to Christian doctrine. Wilhelm Busch and Esther held the same belief: that following Jesus was the first and most primary element of Christianity—the rest being just fluff and often distraction. I began to read the book over a few weeks. It was a short book and written in simple language.

I already had so many ideas swirling in my head from the past few years: my love of nature and acknowledgment of a Creator; my respect for Cortés and the demotion of Neil Young's view of pre-Christian Aztec paradise; the miracle in Europe, where I was given money I desperately needed at the Minster Cathedral; all the European paintings I had seen, showing heaven and hell— the punishments for sinners and the joys for following God; my respect for the madman Don Quixote with his love for the Church, purity, and Dulcinea; my understanding of God as a hidden Jokerman from Bob Dylan's music; my view of the nature of sex leading to childbirth; my friends' dogmatic, close mindedness to Catholicism, when they were otherwise open to the universe; my reading of an incredible radical, Jesus, who like me, was opposed to an overly rigorous piosity and the commercialization of his time; my fear of the end of the world; and my work dressing vines, which directly paralleled events from the Bible.

All of this was coming to a head in my mind as I read this book. Busch was stating what I had already started to believe: that Jesus was the way to God and that he was the Son of God. But I was confused by my new growing faith in Jesus. My faith was just mine. I still was not sure I wanted to take any final step to declare myself as a true believer in Christ.

As I finished this small book, the final chapter specifically addressed the question of how do I walk with God? Busch replied that I must fully surrender my life to Jesus, and at that moment I will walk with God. I was being asked to make a very profound choice: to abandon my will to Jesus Christ and to stand with him.

42. The Brass Crucifix

I then had a brass crucifix about twelve inches long. From where I obtained it or why I had it, I have no idea. It appeared to have been attached to a gravestone at one time. Perhaps I had found it in the Evergreen Cemetery in Roanoke as a teenager and had carried it with me all this time, thinking it valuable. I just don't know. But nonetheless, I had it in my possession and still have it today. It surprises me that I have not lost it as I have not tried to keep possession of it (until recently). It just stays with me.

As I finished *Jesus: Our Destiny,* I decided that it was time I made a choice. I took hold of that brass crucifix with both hands, and I got on my knees, finally deciding that I would follow Jesus as the Son of God. I would follow him, even if (like Don Quixote) I did not see reality properly, because it was the greatest truth I had come to know: greater than nature, greater than Buddhism, greater than spirituality. I had always believed in a Creator; I was never an atheist. I had come to believe in his existence years earlier, watching trees grow and wondering from where came the first seed. But now I also loved this man Jesus, considering him to be one and the same as the Creator; and I believed he would provide me a safe refuge to heaven and happiness.

As I knelt there, these thoughts flowing through my mind, I wept uncontrollably.

Now I had found a pathway in life and a man to follow. I wanted to be honorable like Don Quixote. I wanted to treat women with dignity and respect. I wanted to stop having sex without marriage. I made a sort of wager with God. I cried to him, "I am not sure about the Christian story, but it makes the most sense from what I grew up with and, more importantly, from what I have discovered the past few years." I thought, perhaps Islam or Buddhism was also a valid way to follow God, but I knew and loved Jesus. I could accept him. I was not convinced by other spiritual narratives, other than my mother-earth theories, but they no longer provided answers to all my questions.

I wanted to be rewarded in life and death. I wanted God to know that even if I was wrong, I was doing the best I can in following Jesus. I would follow him despite the limitations of my mind. He, being God, would understand that I used the best judgment I could to come to him. And, what did I have to lose by following him? It seemed I had nothing to lose except sex, that one sin that now abused my conscience. I feared sex would lead me to hell as I had seen so many lost to sexual desire. Instead, I had much to gain. I wanted to grow to my full potential and to be free to follow the great beauty I had only begun to see. I wanted real and eternal happiness.

I wept for hours in this trance of love and grace. I had finally made up my mind and hung the cross on my wall. I knelt before the cross and wrote:

> *Jesus hanging there on my wall, you shine more light in this room than I will ever need, shining enough light for ten million men.*
> *Jesus, you are my south-facing window.*
> *You alone bring forth healing rays of peace and serenity.*
> *Even at dusk, when the early sun falls, the Son is here to gather around.*

As the hours passed, kneeling before the Lord, I felt crazy, like Don Quixote: What am I doing? But I knew without hesitation that I was assured, being cradled in the Lord's arms.

> *Lord God, my God, beautiful God, only God in heaven,*
> *I will always love you; my love can only be for you.*
> *I rejoice in my pain; this I deserve in your name.*
> *My pain cannot compare to the suffering you have endured.*
> *This whole world is yours, and we are finally together.*
> *I praise you because you are alive and breathing life into your people.*
> *You need love and have for millions of years, and I can give it to you.*
> *I will give it to you. I will give you what you created.*

43. Standing Up to the World

I thought it was possible that I might be wrong: perhaps when I die there will be nothing and my body will naturally seep into the soil as fertilizer, as I had often thought before. But it seemed a much better wager to bet on Jesus as the Son of God than on Mother Earth or my oracles like Neil Young. I had listened to Neil Young as a prophet of nature, of Mother Earth, and environmentalism. I knew all of the lyrics and experienced ecstatic moments listening to him. I had other *prophets* as well: Bob Dylan, Pink Floyd, David Bowie, and others. I had divined every word of their music, seeking messages. But now that I was giving my life to Jesus Christ, I knew I had to destroy all of the music I had. Much of their music had overcome my passions; led me to my glorifying sex, drugs, running away, and rejecting God. Now I had to deny them. I began breaking all of my tapes and albums and stuffing them in a bag.

Suddenly, the sound of a car came rolling up in my driveway. It was my girlfriend, Martha. I jumped up off my knees, hid the bag that contained the destroyed music tapes, wiped the tears from my face, and ran out. I hoped to prevent her from coming inside, finding me in that state of prayer and grace, weeping. I hurriedly said hello, not looking at her, so that she would not see on my face what I had just experienced. I felt as if my face was beaming out like Moses after having come out from behind the burning bush, and I didn't want her to know or see that. Acting nonchalantly to fool her, I told her that I was on my way out. She asked, "Where are you going?" I said, "I am heading to the forest to cruise." Moving quickly, without regard to her feelings, I got on my bike and took off. I did not have the courage to tell her about my conversion. I was too addicted to sex and too ashamed to tell her I was Christian.

I headed into the Finger Lakes National Forest, just ten minutes away, the same place that I had attended the Rainbow Gathering earlier. But now I was here after having given my life to Jesus. As I drove my motorcycle deeper into the forest, I grew angry at myself for my cowardly act of running away. I was yelling at myself in my helmet, "Why are you so afraid!?" I dismounted my bike on a gravel path called Chicken Coop Road and made my way onto a trail I had walked on in the past. I walked up to an old cow gate, leaned upon it, and looked down at the meadow and across the plains. I gazed at this pastoral view while praying: "I have no rational arguments left, Lord." I asked, "What on earth should I do now? I love you, Lord, but I am torn between you and human love."

Just then, as I leaned on the gate, I remembered having read the Gospel of John, where Jesus said, "I am the gate. Whoever enters by me will be saved, and will come in and go out and find pasture" (John 10:9). Standing at that old cow gate, I knew the Lord was opening the gate for me now. He was standing right in front of me.

I walked on some more, without purpose or aim, around trees and a pristine pond, through brush, away from the modern world. As I walked, I wished that I could walk with the Lord in the forest forever. Away from all the distractions of the world and the flesh, just nature and the Lord.

But I knew I couldn't. I had to face up to the world, starting with Martha. It was time to follow God entirely without reservation. Time to pronounce Jesus as the one I love and follow. It was time to stop hiding him. It was time I paid what I owed. I promised to follow him no matter what: to improve my life, to live with dignity, to go back to school and make something of my life, and to stay away from sex until marriage. I wanted to follow the words of Jesus Christ.

I got on my bike and rode back home. I was shaking with fear, but I knew Jesus was with me, giving me strength. A tremendous monster was coming out of me as I stood up to all I knew—to my past decade of sin. Martha was still waiting for me. I walked directly up to her, and it all came out of me. I told her, "I am breaking up with you because I cannot have a sexual relationship anymore. I am a follower of Jesus. I gave my life to Christ. I am now a Christian." Martha was baffled but did not lose her confidence or poise. She quietly left. But she was not ready to wholly abandon me yet, as I would soon discover.

I gave my life to Christ in April of 1991. I had just turned twenty-two a few weeks earlier.

I continued journaling most days and wrote this prayer:

> *You gave me life: I disgraced it.*
> *You gave me love: I abused it.*
> *You gave me a mind: I destroyed it.*
> *You gave me a family: I abandoned it.*
> *Now I give this life to you, O Lord.*

Now I give this love I feel.
These feelings I have never felt: I give them back to you.
Praise the Lord, Son of God, praise him with all that is within
*   me.*
Together, we can overcome hatred.
Together, we can live a holy life in love.
Oh Jesus! I wish every man and woman gave you the love
*   you have given me,*
So you can feel how beautiful it is!

44. Pascal's Wager

At that time, I did not then know who Blaise Pascal was. I would learn years later about this seventeenth-century French philosopher, skeptic, mathematician, physicist, inventor, and writer. Looking back on my conversion (having since read much more), it appeared that it similarly followed his theory called *Pascal's Wager*. This wager holds that it is in one's best interest to behave and act as if God exists since the possibility of heaven is far better than eternal punishment in hell:

> God is, or he is not. But to which side shall we incline? Reason can decide nothing here. There is an infinite chaos which separates us. A game is being played at the extremity of this infinite distance where heads or tails will turn up. What will you wager? . . . Since you must choose, let us see which interests you least. You have two things to lose, the true and the good; and two things to gain, your reason and your will, your knowledge and your happiness; and your nature has two things to shun, error and misery. . . But your happiness? Let us weigh the gain and the loss. . . If you gain, you gain all; if you lose, you lose nothing. Wager, then, without hesitation that he is.[22]

My personal wager was similar including the idea that it was in my own best interest to live on earth in a noble and dignified way, pursuant to the Christian principles of faith, love, and dignity, rather than to follow the baser earthly ideas of my organic, natural-earth philosophy.

I didn't have full certitude of what lies behind that great veil of mystery. Perhaps reality was entirely different from what appeared to my mind and eyes, but I wanted to follow Jesus as a safe harbor, a refuge for my unknowing. Not only did I want to avoid the pangs of hell and find paradise upon death, but I wanted to enjoy a good healthy life on this planet, not one of drugs, multiple sex partners, guilt, depression, divorce, and pain. So much of what I had already suffered in my life was self-imposed. I wanted to take away my self-imposed pain and live a good, honorable life, as Don Quixote had done, even if it was all madness.

As I made my wager, the ideas espoused in Dylan's *Jokerman* weighed heavily on me. I thought that since God is hidden from sight to the modern world and shows himself differently to various religions, that it was hard to see him for who he really is. But if I take a bet, using my best judgment, I can follow the manifestation of God and park myself in that safe harbor, knowing that God will accept me if I have a clear conscience, choosing to the best of my ability.

Making this simple wager also helped me to overcome what would have likely been a significant stumbling block. If someone were to have asked me to become a Catholic, I would have laughed them off. I didn't want to follow that religion of my father, with its massive amounts of rules, even if I had come to agree with some of its teachings. But to only say, "Yes, I will follow you, Jesus, because I love you," was a more natural declaration. I was a Christian, and the rest was ancillary.

45. Seeking Denominations

The book *Jesus: Our Destiny* advised that once one gives his life to Christ, he should then find fellowship with other Christians. This was Busch's centrality of Jesus' message; denominations were not so important, one's decision is primary, but then share the faith with others. Typically, one just looks for a congregation that feels suitable.

That Sunday, I drove my motorcycle to Ithaca to attend church for the first time in over ten years . . . but the very first time willingly. I knew a church in Ithaca that I used to walk by every day. It had a large striking red door in the middle of its traditional architecture and a high steeple, which reminded me of the grandeur of European churches. The name was St. John's. It was Episcopalian, but I didn't realize that at the time. I didn't care what kind of denomination it was. I went because it was a beautiful Christian church, traditional looking, and I knew its location.

As soon as I walked in, I felt a familiarity. As a child, my father would bring me to Catholic churches for mass. He would often point to a box in the center of the church at the altar and whisper to me that "Jesus lives in that box." When I entered St. John's, I remembered this when I saw the box in the center, surrounded by beautiful plants, candles, and sacred objects. This was the tabernacle.

I sat up front during the service and could not hold back tears. I tried to keep my emotions in check since everyone was calm and collected. I still had my long hair (though tied in a ponytail) and wore dirty boots and jeans. The entire congregation was older greying men and women, all dressed in a socially proper way. I received the communion, not with any qualms as to whether I was worthy since I didn't even know about that. I had been radically saved just a few days earlier. Jesus was with me full and complete—no one could say otherwise.

I had imagined that there were real and radical Christians who had been saved, like me. I knew how Catholics were as a child, boring I thought—after mass the entire church would head for the door and into their cars. But I thought the saved, Bible-believing Christians were a special group, full of peace, joy, and love. I thought they would open their hearts to me immediately. I thought I would now be part of a beautiful new family and be welcomed with open arms as a convert. I was ready to proclaim myself a true Christian to them all. I wanted to tell everyone about my new faith and make new Christian friends.

But it wasn't so. After the service at St. John's, no one welcomed me. No one said anything to me. Everyone just left. In fact, many people looked at me in a scolding way as if I didn't belong there. I did not feel welcome. But I went up to talk to the priest, who I believe was a bishop, and told him: "I am a new Christian: I have given my life to Jesus." He said unenthusiastically, "Congratulations," but did not care to speak more, saying, "I have to go—nice to meet you." I was let down. But it didn't matter. I didn't need approval. It took me so many years to come to this. For so long I had been a runaway, a thief, a drug user, a radical environmentalist, and had been directly opposed to Christianity. Now I was a Christian through and through and didn't need any validation. I never went back there. I remembered what Wilhelm Busch said, that one should continue to look for a denomination until finding one that feels right.

As I left the church, I went walking in Ithaca, and I came across an event organized by a New Age group. There had been a big party the night before, and, as usual, there was empty beer cans and trash leftover. This group was the party hippies (not the intellectuals) of Ithaca: those who take psychedelic drugs, the light healers, the witches of light and wizards, and just plain vagabonds living in their cars. These were similar to those I met at the Rainbow Gathering.

I had begun to fear this strange population after the dream I had of falling to the earth. I imagined they had some evil energy, somehow being swayed by the devil. I had always tried to avoid black magic and the dark arts. I knew the devil was real now. But now my fear of him, and those who appeared swayed by him, was gone. As a Christian, I felt a new step in my gait. I was walking confidently, together with Jesus. I simply walked by this New Age event without concern. I had no desire to follow false gods anymore, and I had no fear of their subtle and sometimes evil ways. Evil no longer held sway over me. The devil no longer scared me.

The next Sunday I tried a new church, the Assembly of God. This was a much different experience, much friendlier. After the service, everyone would meet and talk. It was what I had imagined fellowship would be like. But then I noticed a new feeling in me. I was not ready to proclaim myself a new Christian from the top of my voice as I had thought. Instead, I was shy in talking with others in the large church group. I was surrounded by people that appeared much more pious and refined than myself. I was afraid to speak as I imagined I might accidentally offend someone. I knew I never had much training in social mores, restraint, and grace. I would talk to them but not for too long since I was afraid to say something out of place. I was still a hippie, though cleaned up, but now I was one in love with Jesus. After ten years of running (almost like a wild animal), I felt shy among these people. It was as if I began to see myself as no longer liberated (as Adam felt after eating the apple), and I felt shame for who I had been.[23]

But the youth pastor there was very kind. He befriended me and invited me to stay at his home with his wife and children for an evening. I enjoyed getting to know them, so I decided to go back the following Sunday.

That second Sunday a film was shown. It depicted the *Rapture,* as they called it. I knew about the Armageddon in the book of Revelation since fear of it was part of the reason I became a Christian. But the film's interpretation bothered me. It showed that in the last days only those whose name was written in what they called the *Book of Life* would be saved. The rest were cast out. I would later learn that the Assembly of God Church officially interprets Revelation 21:27 (and other biblical chapters) to hold this doctrine. The film angered me since it seemed to take away the free choice I had just exercised in choosing Jesus. I could not imagine a God being bound by some predestined book, taking away free will to accept or reject him. I felt that despite the youth pastor's kindness, this wasn't the congregation for me. I went on looking for another community.

In the following days, I decided to tell others about my new life. I told my brother Patrick that I had become a Christian. He was confounded; he thought it was just a phase I would grow out of. I also wrote Esther a letter, informing her that I had become a Christian and thanking her for having encouraged and influenced me. My feelings for her were complicated and uncertain as I started to wonder whether I felt love for her or just admiration and thanks. I then called my father; I told him, "I am sorry for all the pain I caused you. I am now a Christian." He could barely believe it. "Oh, okay," he said. He was happy, but I could hear in his voice that he doubted me. But I didn't care because I knew what I had done. He later confided in me that he then thought I would never have become a Christian; it was a complete shock to him as I had so firmly opposed religion and Christianity.

That week I was to burn everything from my past life: clothing, all my previous writings (except one book of old poems), drawings I called mind lines (surrealist scribblings), matchbooks, pamphlets, cards, messages, different odds and ends, and, of course, all of my music. Music had been like heroin for me—so powerful and addictive. I felt that if I didn't stop listening, it would be the primary reason my soul would land in hell. It would seduce me. I wrote in my new journal, "Deliver me from the devil's radio so that I can see the peace of your rocking chair, the chair of eternal life, instead of rocking my soul right to hell." I was not going to fill my mind with tempting lyrics anymore. Somehow, I innately knew what Aristotle (not yet having even heard of him) had written 2,500 years earlier, that music can overpower the souls of some.

Thus, everything went into great big boxes. Then, just outside of my cottage, I lit a massive fire, burning it all into an ash heap; my own personal *Bonfire of the Vanities*. At this time, too, I stopped smoking cigarettes and marijuana, drinking, and sex. I went cold turkey. I was a new man, born again.

During those early days of my conversion, I relied on God and wrote profusely in my new journal: "If God adorns me with the wonderful art of writing, I will graciously accept and will always remember why I am writing and who gave me the mind capable of loving him." I continued one morning in May:

> *There is a fine mist huddling over the ground. It is the morning I work in the garden. The sun quickly dissipates the moisture.*
>
> *After an hour of gardening, which I dearly love, it is time to be quiet with God: to listen to his words and read his psalms, to play my guitar and read my prose to him, to sit peacefully, sipping water so that I, like the earth and soil, will be nourished with moisture from the Great Spirit that is here.*
>
> *Every morning I know that God loves the world. He sends up the sun and sends away my laziness, just as he sends away*

the moon and stars. The great sun is so powerful and yet so gentle.

By God, I am no longer the poor lost soul I've always been. Jesus is ever present now. The Holy Ghost is always here, and God himself is great because he has given me peace on earth.

Just then, I looked to the sky and saw a great light. And since I believed, was taken from this wretched earth to never see the likes of it again; to never feel the pain or the pressure to give in.

Since I wholeheartedly believed what is, and will always be, the truth, and did not misuse or twist his commandments, I will now enter into the kingdom of the most high: The Kingdom of God!

46. Essenes, Temptation & Doubt

I also told my neighbor Preston about my new faith. He didn't accept it, wanting to make his protest known. Being a Marxist and Darwinist, he tried to convince me that Christianity was no longer as important as it once had been. He said, "In the modern world, man's intellect has evolved beyond the need for faith and religion," continuing, "Man has evolved such that he constantly becomes smarter. The world will be far more advanced soon." He argued that today, "God is dead, and now man is God."

I responded to him the best I could, using my newfound Christianity, mixed with my earlier views of environmentalism (journaling it later):

> *Don't you see how far behind we have put our future generations, with all the so-called advances of the past decade: pollution, radioactive waste, day care centers, chemicals we put in our bodies, and trash dumps everywhere. What have we left for our children? A playground of wooden spikes and steel, full of pitfalls, lacking the joys of pure nature. You think the way we have ruined the planet shows how much smarter we are than God? God is far more advanced than the small abilities of man.*

But, of course, Preston was my landlord, friend, and neighbor. I didn't want to argue, but I wouldn't be convinced of his faith in progress, in opposition to the divine.

Preston was on friendly terms with my girlfriend Martha. After my conversion, she would often come to visit Preston and his family, hoping to see me. Once she came to my door and let it be known that she still wanted to be with me. She said, "I understand you and respect your conversion. But why does it mean we can't be together anymore?" She wanted to be with me even as a Christian, and she was now even willing to leave her other boyfriend for me. She thought we could get married.

She brought me a book to read: it was *The Essene Gospels*, purportedly Christian writings based on original Hebrew and Aramaic texts, translated and edited by Edmond Bordeaux Szekely. Martha said, "This book will help you in your new faith." It struck my curiosity, and I was grateful for her gift. I began to read it. In it, I read about how Jesus had supposedly lived for a short time with a Jewish ascetical sect called the Essenes, teaching them doctrines that differed from the Gospels in the Bible. For example, Jesus taught that the Earthly Mother is above all creation—our flesh and blood coming from her. He also taught the Essenes how to clean their bowels with enemas, believing that the sacred flushing of them would rid the body of toxic impurity and sin. Jesus would speak of kneeling before the angel of water and inserting the stalk of a gourd into one's *hinder parts*, letting the water flow, thereby ridding the body of Satan.

Martha wanted me to understand that the way some traditional Christians understood Christianity was incorrect. She believed that I could stay a follower of Jesus and still live a lifestyle outside of the traditionally accepted morality of Christianity and more in line with how I had been living, according to the ways of nature and Mother Earth. The book was in alignment with her (and my) organic lifestyle. Jesus was more concerned with toxins in the body that separated us from his grace. Personal sin didn't include such things as sex since sex was natural for men and women to engage in.

I was thoroughly uncertain and troubled; it was so radically different than the four Gospels I had read, as well as the entire New Testament, yet it was supposedly contemporaneous. I wanted to be with Martha. I wanted to marry her, too. Now I was single, without sex and the warmth of a woman I had grown accustomed to. My doubts began to take over my body and mind and started in at my soul. I wrote:

> *Jesus, hang on to me, even though you are the one I am now trying to lose. You know I am tired, Lord. You know my strength has been tested and has failed. The things that I have done and those I've thought. The careless life I've led. I am always putting my life at risk. I act in vain—whatever I do outside of you. I feel worthless, yet I know my life is precious to you since I am made in your image.*

More doubts kept coming. I read a popular magazine which stated, "The Bible was surely not written by any of the disciples, Matthew, Mark, Luke or

John, not even while they were alive." It continued, "The biblical phrase *Jesus was born of the Holy Spirit* was only a way of expression during the time the books were written; there were others of the time that were also thought to be *born of the Holy Spirit*."

This magazine and the *Essene Gospels* rattled my faith. Why shouldn't I go back with Martha? Now I could see there was much uncertainty about what Jesus taught. But was I saved only by what I read in the Bible? Is the Bible the only authority for Christianity? No, I thought. For me, there was so much more, such as conscience and grace. I did not define Jesus and God by the written word only. For me, he was much bigger than that.

The song *Jokerman* again came to my mind. Yes, God seems to hide himself. Why isn't he more explicit as to who he is and what he wants from man? Yet asking these old questions upset me. I thought I had already overcome them. I began to ask Jesus to help me understand and accept.

I now believed in Jesus as the Son of God and someone I would follow. But I admitted to myself that much of modern Christianity might possibly be false. I imagined that many men and women had reworked and edited the words spoken by Jesus over the 2,000 years since his death. I wondered how much had been altered. I made no claims that my mind could determine truth amid falsity. I doubted I could come to definitive truth because of this. I knew there were a million books in the world, each with a different perspective, and that at least some authors had likely lied and twisted the truth.

I was only ready to claim one thing: ignorance. I was ready to be a fool, but one for Christ. I must be like Job, I thought. I will believe no matter how much doubt I feel. I will trust that God will allow me passage through the gate if I do my best to understand and accept him in this great mystery of life.

Long-term, I knew that I would have to fight to keep my faith. I knew that my own mother had fallen away from her faith after her suicide attempt. I imagined she had fallen away because she lacked true knowledge of the faith, just as Jesus taught in the parable of the sower about the new seedlings: ". . . when the sun rose, they were scorched; and since they had no root, they withered away" (Matthew 13:6). I wanted my garden to withstand the elements of nature and, therefore, knew I needed to educate myself. I wrote in my journal:

Today the forces of evil were upon me. I will fix my eyes on the light. I will never turn away. I will be paralyzed by its glare before I look away from your stare. I tell you that what I believe cannot be read, cannot be imagined, and cannot be lived up to. I can only live my life the best I know how, only with your help, no one else's. I do not attempt to understand you, Lord. My mind can only think silly human thoughts. You have complete dominion. You don't even have to listen to me. But forgive me for my faults and sins, because they are many. I need so much, Lord. Help me to fashion my life to your liking so that you are happy with me. I ask for much: please understand me. Show me if these things are right in your eyes.

As a new Christian, I often thought about my mother. Why had she tried to commit suicide? It's sad her new faith did not prevent this, I thought. Would I ever face so much pain? Would doubt and pain grow so strong in me that I, too, would suffer this temptation? I knew that my mind was far from perfect: I had abused drugs, ran away from home, and lived a dissolute life. I believed that it was likely I was psychologically imbalanced. My time in Straight and my meetings with psychologists would prove my imbalance if I let it. But I decided to rely on God to give me the grace to overcome my fears, doubts, deep pain, and even my deep-seated fear of suicide.

I wrote a vision I had in my journal. It was similar to the dream I had as a youth, of chasing a deer through the forest on a hunt—only to let him go out of the love of nature he had shown me. This new vision was to help those who faced suicidal tendencies, including most especially myself. It was a preemptive strike against my own self-doubt and even hatred for the things I had done. I knew I was in God's grace, but I needed a way out if things ever got too bad. It was my own escape to Bolivia as *Butch Cassidy and the Sundance Kid* had done (in the movie my mother had shown me as a child):

Can I make a request of you, you who want to kill yourself?
I ask you to leave the city any way you can.

When you leave, go to the mountains and climb the highest one.
When you reach the top, look for the best place to jump.
While there, think about yourself and your life.
Now on the peak, there should be a view, but the fog is obscuring it.
Yet imagine how beautiful it would be under the fog.
Now look down and see the rocks which will crush your bones,
And look up to see the many vultures circling in the air.
Before you jump, I ask you to listen carefully.
Imagine jumping off to rid yourself from this terrible existence,
Yet still be able to live on, in peace and serenity.
Well, my friend, it can be done.
Don't allow your body to jump. No, throw down your heart, throw down your pain, throw down your insecurities, throw down your crazy past, but keep your body.
You can do this with Jesus Christ.
The devil will catch your past, your pain.
Do not throw your body down as the devil will catch that, too.
The things which belong to the devil, he may take.
The things which belong to Almighty God will be preserved.
He will not neglect you but will protect and defend you.
You can trade the evil eating at your heart for beautiful gifts:
A clean soul, a brilliant mind, a healthy body.
A robust life, whole and true, will be given to you.
God will sit with you on that mountain, with your body and mind so limp and tired.
He will rock you in his arms; he will swing the gate open to your eternal peace.
And you shall see, as you walk down the mountain with God . . . that thick fog is lifting.

In the end, despite my near despair, neither the *Essene Gospels,* nor the magazine, nor my desire for Martha, were convincing enough to alter my new faith. I was no biblical scholar, but the four Gospels seemed more authentic than the *Essene Gospels.* The Gospels had continuity with the Old Testament, I thought. I believed that Jesus was continuing and expanding on Moses' Ten Commandments; murder and theft were all still outlawed as was sexual relations outside of marriage. No one had ever spoken of our Earthly Mother in the Bible before or washing sins out through the bowels. Jesus' teachings were not about the health of the body but love and the eternity of the soul. Having read the entire Bible had helped weed out my doubts. St. Paul himself warned the early Christians: ". . . I am afraid that as the serpent deceived Eve by its cunning, your thoughts will be led astray from a sincere and pure devotion to Christ" (2 Corinthians 11:3).

47. Infatuation or Love?

My early conversion was a moment of pure grace, yet those few weeks after were full of grave doubts and discouragements. I had not even found a suitable fellowship yet. During this time I received a new letter from Esther, which usually raised my spirits. She wrote to congratulate me on becoming a Christian, writing, "I feel somewhat responsible for your salvation." Yes, it was true, very much so, and I thanked her. Yet I feared also. My mother converted for my father, but then she left her faith when their love failed. Her motives were for marriage, I thought, not for herself. I did not want any outside motivations for my faith. I began to distrust my reasons for coming to Jesus as they felt too intimately connected to Esther.

Before my salvation, I was always on the lookout to meet a new sex partner or girlfriend. My love of women had always confused me. For now, I just wanted to prove to myself that I could love God alone without the influence of a woman. I began to think that I should end my friendship with her. I drafted a letter telling her goodbye. I wanted to trust myself and God only. But I could not bring myself to send it. She was my one and only Christian friend. But my feelings were becoming an infatuation. I began to think about her day and night, writing in my journal: "Lord I need to be with her. I need to trust her and love her and give her happiness." I could not control my feelings for Esther. I didn't want this obsession. I wrote, "Lord, I prefer to be addicted to your bread and wine than to any woman."

But I had to imagine, is it possible to love her? It must be. I wrote:

> I know there is a vast ocean of time between her and I. But I must first gain a long-standing stable relationship with you, Lord. Each day I realize that strength is growing in me—serenity and real peace. When will this infatuation end? I give all these thoughts to you; take them. I want to know your will.

48. The Prodigal Son

One morning at the end of spring I received a letter from Brooklyn College. They had accepted me! A high school dropout admitted to Brooklyn College! I bounced around my little cottage with my heart full of pride and joy. The sun was shining outside my cottage and inside my heart that day. But it was not free. I would have to take out student loans and move to New York City. I was ready but uncertain. Could I survive the sexual temptations that would inevitably come living alone in New York City? Or, could I be stable as to stay in one place and study? My heart felt so much wilder than the density and cement of city life.

Maybe I needed to choose something more radical. What of my love of *seeing the world?* It was still in my mind. My imagination was spinning, as it often had. I began to wonder if I should be an itinerant preacher. I loved to travel, and now I thought I could go on foot throughout the country preaching the gospel. I imagined myself like the Bob Dylan song *Man in the Long Black Coat,* which is about an itinerant man listening to sermons and walking through Africa. My tapes were all destroyed, but my mind still carried all the lyrics. Perhaps it was my calling to carry the Bible, preaching and walking, while wearing just an old coat. It would be a sort of rambling for God. It would be my own Don Quixote sally. I had found God by rambling, I thought, so now I could bring God to others by rambling. I didn't want to be fashionable and cool: I just wanted to serve him.

But this idea seemed to have as many problems as the idea of moving to New York City for school. I knew that my budding faith needed not only education but protection if I was to keep it. Moving to New York City would undoubtedly lead to significant temptations, as would rambling alone in the world with only a Bible. In both instances, I would not be nourishing and developing my faith. I wanted to protect my faith as a new young oak tree in the forest: "Like a baby oak tree you planted me with careful hands; but a baby oak is vulnerable to harsh climates and careless animals," I wrote—similar to a passage I had read in the New Testament: "I planted, Apollos watered, but God gave the growth" (1 Corinthians 3:6).

I called my father to tell him about being accepted into Brooklyn College and about my idea of becoming an itinerant preacher. He agreed that my faith needed education and protection. He offered (without my asking or expecting), if I was serious about my life now, that I could come live with him and that he would pay for me to attend the University of Cincinnati. However, if I chose to go to Brooklyn College, he would not pay. He was giving me an incentive to live with him. The only proviso was that there would be no drinking, smoking, or poor communication. For me, this was easy, because now I had faith. I wrote, "I have faith in my decision through Jesus Christ. I believe he is not leading me astray. Whatever the outcome is, I pray I will remain faithful. Paranoia for an unknown future is the least of my worries. God will have his way with me."

I liked this idea of living with my father while going to school and for not having to take student loans. But what of all the bad memories of my father: of his negativity, the times he put me in Straight, handcuffed me, and grounded me for months on end?

God seemed to be showering grace on me as I no longer had concern for those memories. At that moment God helped me to truly forget my negativity toward him. Before this, I had always felt that he was one of the most significant impediments to my becoming a Christian. I resented the way he raised me, continually speaking of Catholicism and being negative to any and all other ways of life. I didn't want to be as his St. Anthony in the Desert painting suggested, living alone in a cave. I didn't want to have his limited vision of the world, not dreaming, with no desire to see the world. I was his complete opposite. I loved the world and wanted to see all of it. I didn't look like him, taking much more after my mother and her father. He had little sense of art, where my mother had developed in me a love of art. It's almost as if I had no respect for him before becoming Christian. I tried as much as possible to differentiate myself. One way of doing this was to rebel against his religion. But now, I was convinced of Christianity *in spite of him*. I had come to God, not because he wanted it or because of some program like Straight. I came to God on my own—as an adult, entirely free, and completely independent of him. And I was not a Catholic; I was simply a Jesus-believing Christian.

Now, none of this was at the forefront of my mind. I only authentically wanted to see him. In those moments I had nothing but love for him. This has no other explanation than God's grace in my soul. I had forgotten all about the past, our strains, and problems. I was ready for any new adventure as long as Jesus was with me.

In June of 1991, I left Ithaca for Cincinnati and moved into my father's house. I wrote:

> *I have packed my bags the best I know how for the long journey down the road of Christianity. If I have forgotten anything from my old home, so be it. I will find everything I need ahead. The light of day that God has brought forth in me I will radiate back to the Lord.*

I was now a prodigal son, having left my sinful life, returning to the house of my father. I had never intended this, but it was a natural progression. Everything began changing rapidly. I started to dress well, grooming myself and cutting my hair a little shorter. I was immediately admitted into the remedial night school at the University of Cincinnati. I was taking general courses, rethinking what I wanted as a profession. I enjoyed English literature courses and geography.

After a semester, having done well in my classes, I applied to the day school's Bachelor of Arts program. To my great surprise, I was accepted. It was a massive source of pride for me as it was a much bigger and more prestigious school than Brooklyn College. I had come a long way in a very short time.

The program was to begin in the fall, but I decided to defer until the winter quarter because Esther and I were continuing our writing and had decided it was time to finalize our relationship, to find out what the next step would be. I felt eternally in her debt for the gift of faith. But did I love her for marriage or only for this gift? I was not at peace but wanted it. I bought a plane ticket to Germany for the month of October 1991. I was invited to stay in her family's home.

I called my mother. I had delayed telling her about my faith for a few long weeks as I knew she didn't care for Christianity. But it was time. I told her about my new life of faith, my new education, and my new love interest. She was happy for me to have found dignity and self-respect and was overjoyed that I was attending the university. Even though she was not a practicing Christian, she was happy that I had converted, but she cautioned me to not become over-zealous. She would later send me a Bible that Thomas Jefferson had assembled. He had cut away all extraneous teachings, focusing only on the words of Jesus.[24] He cut and paste from the New Testament books, excluding nearly all the miracles and talk of the divinity of Jesus. My mother preferred I follow Jesus as a great teacher, as Jefferson had done, not in formal religion.

She then gave me some advice regarding Esther. I told her I had a hard time concentrating on my studies thinking about her. She said, "If you do not feel peace, she is probably not the one for you." It was sad to hear, but it felt true. I would not forget these words.

49. The Rock of Peter

It was still summer of 1991, and I had to wait a few months to see Esther. During these few months living with my father, we had frequent conversations about Christianity and its origins and history. He knew much about the Bible and was not overbearing with his views (perhaps age had softened him). He kept telling me, "I accept you where you are." This was all I needed from him. Our conversations about Christianity were one-on-one, man-to-man, not father-to-child.

He began to tell me his opinions on the authority of the pope: that Jesus chose Peter as the first pope, and this pope was his vicar on earth. He pointed out several scriptural passages to support this. When I re-read the New Testament in this light, the idea of Peter being Jesus's vicar made immediate sense:

> And I tell you, you are Peter, and on this rock I will build my church, and the gates of Hades will not prevail against it. I will give you the keys of the kingdom of heaven, and whatever you bind on earth will be bound in heaven, and whatever you loose on earth will be loosed in heaven" (Matthew 16:18–19).

It appeared clear that Jesus granted to Peter the keys to this new Christian religion and intended for him to carry on the authority of Jesus on earth. But were these keys for the religion Catholicism? My father then presented me with a historical chart, showing every pope since Peter, a line of apostolic succession in the Catholic Church that has never been broken in the 2,000 years since Jesus died. This was compelling evidence.

Since converting, I had been continually looking for a denomination to join; each sect or branch I went to seemed to be different in their interpretation of the Bible, at least in part. I recalled being angry watching the video in the Assembly of God Church that showed how only those in the *Book of Life* would be saved, whereas in the Bible I read that Jesus could save anyone.

In Cincinnati, I had found a church I liked soon after moving there, the Salvation Army. I liked it because its attendees were people like me, ramblers, those with family and drug problems, the downtrodden. It was easy to fit in where pride and pomposity were lacking. Also, questions about doctrine were not central. They taught everyone could be saved, even the worst of society. This was much closer to the Jesus I knew who cared for the lost sheep.

But it was hard to ignore that unity in Christianity was broken. In the south of the United States, there were thousands of different sects. When I worked on the dairy farm in Boones Mill, Virginia, the owners belonged to a large sect there called the Dunkard Brethren, who believe in wearing only black clothes and driving black cars. Their name came from the fact that during baptism they must be fully dunked into a river; pouring water over the head is insufficient. It was hard for me to imagine that Jesus had intended so many different sects when he taught what he did. It seemed clear that the sect that existed at the time Jesus died would be the correct one—all the rest being aberrations. This was logical, I thought. The idea of a pope seemed to be the most rational way one would go about ensuring continuity of a new faith. And the fact of the papacy having 2,000 years of apostolic succession gave the idea credibility.

After just a few months talking with my father, I was reasonably convinced that Jesus intended Peter to have authority to bind and continue his church, and I was now wondering if perhaps the Catholic Church was the true church, founded by Jesus himself.

It had taken me my entire life to choose Christianity, most of that time directly opposed to Catholicism, yet now my objections to Catholicism began to fall. Yet I still had many doubts. I didn't understand the role of priests or celibacy. When Jesus spoke of priests, he usually derided them. For example, in the parable of the Good Samaritan, Jesus speaks of a "priest" who walked onto the other side of the road to avoid helping an injured man (Luke 10:31). And it was the priests of his time that doubted him (Mark 11:27–28). Finally, it was the high priest Caiaphas that organized the plot to kill Jesus (John 11:49). The Gospels seemed to portray the priests as Jesus' opponents. Who needed priests to follow Jesus, I thought? They only seemed to get in the way. I never had a sincere respect for them. They were meddlers. I came to believe in Jesus as one radical to another. I still opposed establishments and large organizations. Priests did not even work, I thought. How could I trust that God wanted a group of men (who do not work) to be representative of him?

But my mind was open to Jesus and what he intended, even if some things seemed odd or wrong to my ears. And I slowly began to understand the history and need for priests. I learned that the priesthood involves a consecration to Christ through the sacrament of orders. The idea was the same as Jesus ordaining Peter to be the pope when he gave him the keys. Over time, as the Church grew, there was a need to have help. The pope ordained bishops, who then ordained priests. The priests helped to serve the growing numbers of faithful just as Jesus had served and taught his disciples.

The Catholic Eucharist seemed to be the primary reason for priests. I read the Bible passage which says that Jesus took bread and wine during the Last Supper and gave it to his disciples saying, "Take, eat; this is my body" (Matthew 26:26). The Catholic Church teaches that the bread and wine is miraculously changed into his body and blood. In the Bible, Jesus tells his apostles to, "Do this in remembrance of me" (Luke 22:19). Even though it seemed completely irrational, the Catholic Eucharist was fairly easy for me to accept. As a follower of Jesus, I believed in miracles, having read of so many in the Gospels; therefore, this miracle did not seem too far-fetched. It was easy to accept because the words Jesus used were so clear, he did not use the words *this symbolizes my body and blood*, but this "is." And I began to think it natural that Jesus would intend a specific class of persons to have the duty to perform this miracle of the Eucharist in the mass.

Regarding celibacy of priests and consecrated, this was difficult to understand. Jesus was born into a family of Joseph and Mary. The early apostles had been married. I did not understand the point of it. My father pointed out this passage in the Gospels:

> The unmarried man is anxious about the affairs of the Lord, how to please the Lord; but the married man is anxious about the affairs of the world, how to please his wife, and his interests are divided (1 Corinthians 7:32–34).

My father gave me a book called the *Story of a Soul* by St. Theresa of Lisieux. I could not help but be incredibly moved; it drew me to tears. She had lived a completely different life than me—full of purity, but her simplicity profoundly affected me. I came to learn later that this little book had converted millions. It is hard to understand why it has had such an impact, but it's likely because of her utter simplicity of confidence and love—her little way of abandonment to God's love through small unknown acts. For example, she would pick up another's trash out of love for God, when no one else saw her. I once saw my father do this in the streets of Cincinnati. I was at a distance, so he did not see me, but as he walked down a city street, he picked up a random piece of trash and put it in a bin. I could understand the power of this humble act. Only God sees this declaration of smallness for him.

St. Theresa continued to love all of her superiors and co-sisters in the convent, even though they often treated her poorly. I began to understand that in Christianity people were just the same as everyone else—full of flaws and judgments. I was deeply disappointed when I first converted since no one thought my conversion was important or even real; yet for me, it was the most crucial event in the world. Now I could see that even faithful Christians could be cold, but the fire can remain in my heart, as it did in Little Theresa, as long as I offer even the smallest acts of love for Jesus, sight unseen. She loved Jesus so much that she wanted to give the greatest gift to him, her celibacy. It was an act of love. Her love helped me to understand this idea of celibacy. Little Theresa had ignited my heart to Catholicism.

The only significant problem I had left with Catholicism was the cult of Mary. I didn't understand it. Why did the Catholics love Mary so much? I remember Jesus rebuking Mary in the Bible, calling her "woman" instead of mother, and even telling her his time had not come: "Woman, what concern is that to you and to me? My hour has not yet come" (John 2:4), he said to her when she asked him to perform a miracle at the wedding feast in Cana. Jesus seemed to speak to her derogatorily as if trying to make a point that she was not relevant (and perhaps a distraction) in terms of salvation history.

Yet, Mary's image was everywhere in Catholic churches, and people would fall on their knees to her. I did not see Mary as prominent, and my father could not convince me that the Catholic Church's cult of Mary was correct. But I wasn't ready to give up on Catholicism. I was now very curious.

My father gave me some audio tapes of Scott Hahn, a young Catholic convert. He had been a Protestant minister for many years. He had believed in *sola scriptura*, that the Bible was the sole source of Christian teaching, a common belief for Protestants who reject the authority of tradition and the papacy. But he had concluded that the very Bible itself was assembled under the authority of the Catholic Church in what is called the biblical canon. This would lead to his conversion. It made sense; why would Protestants use a Bible that the Catholic Church had assembled? Why didn't they assemble their own? I remembered reading the *Essene Gospels*; who had authority to exclude them (if they were genuinely ancient documents)? It was the Catholic Church who formed the biblical canon, including some books and excluding others.

Esther, and all the Christians I had met up to that point, believed in *sola scriptura*, that only the Bible could teach man how to live as a Christian. But it was not the Bible alone that led to my conversion; it was my own idea of *Pascal's Wager* and my understanding of a natural law in man. Pure Biblicism was not how I was led to Jesus. In fact, I initially imagined that, over the generations, Jesus' words had been twisted. Hahn spoke about this, too: he would explain that the Bible itself does not err, but that not all that is contained in God's law is contained in the Bible. This helped dispel my doubts that perhaps much of what was written about Christ had been twisted over the generations. No, what was in the Bible was all true, but that there was more than just what was written; there was also an oral tradition, and that is why *sola scriptura* was not sufficient. And for Hahn, this oral tradition necessitated a pope, a guardian and promulgator of teaching.

One of the other main reasons for Hahn's conversion was that he believed the Catholic Church was correct in its stance against contraception. This resonated with me because what I saw as the unnatural use of contraception was one of the main reasons I became a Christian. His conversion to this teaching was much purer than mine in that he was a faithfully married man and I was a single man practicing illicit sex. I was like an animal in a state of nature but with a philosophical questioning mind. Contraception made no sense from an organic natural state, I thought.

My father and Scott Hahn were answering all of my questions about Catholicism versus a simpler Christianity. I was becoming thoroughly convinced of this *one true church*. I still did not understand the devotion to Mary, but I was now willing to overlook it since I was convinced on so many other points. I would merely waive my understanding of Mary for now.

Thus, six months after giving my life to Jesus, becoming his follower, I was now ready to accept the Catholic Church. There were no tears or great drama as when I first became Christian. It was more a realization of truth or of finding my denomination, as Wilhelm Busch had written in *Jesus: Our Destiny*.

Today, I wonder had I not gone to live with my father following my conversion, and instead moved to New York for school or went traveling through Mexico as an itinerant preacher, would I be a Catholic today? I think probably yes; I would have eventually come to learn these apologetic arguments as they are nothing new or unique. They have existed for hundreds and even thousands of years. But looking back, my rapid ascent to Catholicism seemed to be heavily aided more so by experience than by book learning. It wasn't for nothing that I, as a pagan, had come to respect the Church, following my natural agreement with her stance on contraception. My rambling travels in Europe, too, had readied me; it was there I was greeted with love and kindness in the Catholic homes of Lucía and the Houllieres. And, too, it was a Catholic charity that once helped me in Santa Cruz, the St. Francis Soup Kitchen. As well, my heart was ready partly due to my reading the fanciful *Don Quixote* and the adventurous *Conquest of Mexico*, both overflowing with Catholic imagery and virtue.

Thus, it was now official: I enrolled as a catechumenate in the RCIA (Rite of Christian Initiation for Adults) program at St. Peter in Chains Cathedral in Cincinnati. My completion of RCIA would mean that I would be confirmed at the next Easter Vigil. My father was my sponsor. Since I had already been baptized and received my first communion as a child, I didn't have to wait to receive communion. I only needed to go to confession first, which I did, spending several hours preparing for and confessing over ten years of sins. Confession seemed natural to me—an oral pronunciation of what I had done and a request for forgiveness. The priest was just acting on behalf of Christ, not in his own capacity. I believed God had already forgiven me, but this formal step seemed natural and purifying to tell Jesus directly, annunciating real words.

I had many difficulties accepting what the RCIA teacher was having me read, however. I was not seeing the radical Jesus I had encountered in the Gospels. Instead, I was reading the weak and pathetic Christianity I had always reviled before my conversion. That old caricature of Christianity I had imagined was actually being taught. It was as if I was reading coloring books for children. But I continued to read my own books, and I obtained a good spiritual director, a Jesuit at St. Xavier Church, named Fr. Huber.

There was only one problem with my embrace of Catholicism: the timing. I decided to return to the Catholic Church, the compulsory church of my infancy and early childhood, just two weeks before my flight was to depart to Germany for my visit with Esther. I was a Catholic now and Esther a Protestant. I considered canceling the trip, but in the end, I decided to go. She had given so much to me, and I wanted to try. RCIA and school were put on a short hold while I went back to Freiburg im Breisgau.

50. Purity of Love

The place where Esther and I were to meet was symbolic. It would be the courtyard of the Freiburg Minster, in the same place we had met only two years before. I arrived early and prayed inside for over two hours before meeting her. Being a Catholic now, I was surprised to learn (having not known before) the official name of the Minster, that being the Catholic Cathedral of Our Lady. I was in the same church where I encountered a miracle when a stranger gave me fifty Deutschmarks I so desperately needed. While I was sitting there praying before meeting Ester, I witnessed a small marriage taking place inside. In all my life, I had never been to any wedding as I felt that people like me (the wild ones) did not get invited to such events. The symbolism made me cry for want of love.

Esther arrived, and we embraced, happily but awkwardly, and then we proceeded to take the tram to her home. I knew I had to tell her—my heart was worrying so I just blurted it out, "Esther, I became a Catholic two weeks ago." Her entire demeanor changed. It was as if happiness left her. Her bright, radiant smile turned sad. She told me (as her face contorted bitterly) that, "The Catholic Church is a false church, and the pope is the Antichrist, leading millions astray, down to hell." But she soon recovered her composure, confident that I would change back to being as she, a Bible-only-believing Christian.

I spent the next month living in the basement of her family's home. Every day we had long conversations. She was trying to convert me to her Bible-based Christianity, but most of her arguments I already had answers to, from my listening to Scott Hahn. I was trying to convert her to Catholicism, explaining about the history of the papacy, the authority of the biblical canon, of St. Theresa, and so on. She wouldn't hear it. We seemed to be getting nowhere with each other.

Toward the end of my stay, I had two free days alone to travel. I took the train to the south of Germany and walked across a bridge into a small town in Switzerland. There, I found a Catholic church on a hill, overlooking a river, with an enormous eagle statue and sunlit stained glass. I felt the mix of God and wild nature. Somehow, I felt this eagle was an omen from God, assuring me I was home in my faith. Even to this day, whenever I see a bird of prey flying near me, I immediately think that God is reaffirming me.

Later, I headed to the quaint university city of Konstanz, where I stayed a night before returning to Esther's house. On this train ride, I had my first opportunity to think and write about my feelings for Esther:

> *What can one do when one is in love? What can one think of, only of her? Of being with her and watching her smile. Of gazing at her braided hair, which so gently drops down her back. Ever so lovely this small piece of time. Ever so pleasant to be with her. I love her to the ends of the earth, but I love God throughout the universe. I thank you, Lord, with my whole heart for bringing us together, despite our differences. I will thank you for either keeping us together or breaking us apart. Lord, whatever you will do, do it, and I will bless you with a whole heart. But help me overcome my selfishness, my desire for her, my desire for earthly passion, my desire to sin. I need the hope you so graciously give.*

I tried to spiritualize our meeting. I had love for her, primarily because of her role in my conversion to Christianity. Yet our thirty days of discussions had not led me away from Catholicism; in fact, I was more convinced now. Neither of us budged. I was sad to go, but it was time. The words of my mother rang true: "If you do not feel peace, she is probably not the one for you." With Esther, there was always a conflict. But I was not yet ready to accept that God allows people in our lives for one purpose, but often not for another. It was only natural for me to confuse brotherly love for romantic love.

51. A Religious Vocation?

Back in Cincinnati I resumed RCIA but would have to wait two months until university classes began. I had much time to read and reflect. Esther and I kept writing, yet in each letter, we seemed to drift further apart, unable to come up with a plan forward.

I had promised to God that I would forever love her for having helped me to the faith. I had consecrated myself to her. I was waiting for her to visit me or for some sign that things would improve, neither of which was happening.

But after I read the classic work *Troilus and Criseyde* by Chaucer, I finally began to slowly let her go. It is a tale about the death of human love and the transcendence of divine love. Troilus gave his entire heart and soul to his love Criseyde but had to go away for a time. Criseyde promised Troilus she would wait for him. Yet, she was untrue and soon changed her mind. True love had died. Chaucer was to pen the famous proverb: "All good things must come to an end."[25]

I wrote in my journal:

> *How is it that love can surpass all things, yet pierce so deep, as cold steel blades thrusting into the very heart? The moon rises and yet falls so fast again. How can one live in misery, sick for unrequited love? Poor Troilus had never known about Jesus to give his love to, but I do. Is it natural to fall in love? Yes. Then is it not just as natural to fall out of love? Yes. But the Creator designed our very nature to love him and is never untrue. He never falls away; he only ascends with us.*

I was ready to transcend my human love.

I soon read St. Augustine's *Confessions*. Now I had a real role model—someone like me, who had been addicted to sex, yet finally had broken free, turning his life to God. A line he wrote rang true for me while thinking of Esther: "Show me a man who's loved, and I'll show him God."[26]

Of course, I understood that St. Augustine had consecrated himself to God. I asked myself, should I live a celibate life? Fr. Huber pointed out that Mary Magdalene, after her assent to Jesus, renounced her sinful ways and followed

Jesus celibately. I, too, wanted to love Jesus like Mary Magdalene and St. Augustine.

I decided to discern my vocation. My father suggested that I go on a week-long, silent retreat at the Abbey of Gethsemani in Kentucky, which is run by Trappist monks. The Abbey's starkness reminded me of my father's house as a child: a simple home with little regarding art and beauty. At the Abbey, my room had only a hard bed with a crucifix, surrounded by concrete walls and floor. It didn't attract my overly sensuous sense of style.

I found myself wanting to walk about all day, moving my body regularly, not feeling at peace in all-day prayer and meditation. While walking, I remember finding a statue on an outdoor trail on the property. It was a monk on his knees, praying in agony to the Lord. You could see and feel his pain. I related deeply to this statue; I had felt this way since my conversion. I was desperate to keep Jesus close to me, knowing I could fall into sin at any moment. I wrote a poem:

> *Prayer is the feeling of the nails of Christ piercing my own*
> *   hands;*
> *It is giving in to his burning love;*
> *It is the waking hours of the morning ending in a peaceful*
> *   dream—the dream of my soul united to God;*
> *It is hugging our Lady and crying at Christ's cross for all the*
> *   time I wasted;*
> *It is a dream of the Reality that has finally shown its face;*
> *It was always there to see, I only covered my face so not to*
> *   see, and not to be seen.*
> *Prayer is the love in my lungs that pours out in waves into*
> *   his ocean.*

But I was uncomfortable at the Abbey. I did like their mellifluous singing of prayer, and I liked that they emphasized not only prayer but work also. But I did not feel a vocation to this sort of life and left after just two days, completely restless to go. I knew that my heart was too wild to live in this tamed way the rest of my life.

And I didn't trust myself to live celibately; I didn't feel it would be prudent for me to give up my hope for a wife completely. I thought that I would eventually need a woman again. I took heart at St. Paul's words to the Corinthians:

> It is well for a man not to touch a woman. But because of cases
> of sexual immorality, each man should have his own wife and
> each woman her own husband (1 Corinthians 7:1–2).

Fr. Huber later told me, "Sometimes it takes a while for God to unveil his plan." Thereafter I did not give more consideration to becoming a priest or monk. I simply continued to believe in natural life, that Jesus was a son of a family, and that I would eventually need sex again, would marry, and have children.

52. Easter Vigil

I finally started my first semester at the University of Cincinnati day school, enrolling in more geography, English literature, and history courses. I was also working at the Florence Mall across the border in Kentucky. As a teenage runaway years earlier, I would often stop at this mall on my way from Michigan, and it gave me respite when I escaped the handcuffs of Straight. It was near the freeway bridge where I had once spent a cold, sleepless night as a fugitive. Yet now, instead of thumbing on my way to Florida or escaping Straight, I was driving to the Florence Mall to work as a janitor, sweeping floors and wiping ashtrays clean. As I took out the trash and performed my duties, I would meditate on the Lord. I also began to meditate on Mary. I had slowly started to fall in love with her. Realizing the name of the Freiburg Minster as the Cathedral of Our Lady had been a pleasant surprise. It began to feel natural to honor Mary as the mother of Jesus, and since Jesus was God, this would make her the mother of God. Initially, to become a Catholic, I had to waive the doubts I had about Mary since I did not intellectually understand the attention given to her, but now those doubts were rapidly and miraculously disappearing.

Around this time I got a call from Ithaca. It was my brother Patrick and his friend Sebastian. Sebastian was quite shocked I had become a Catholic. Yet he surprised me when he said, "I am a lapsed Catholic; my mother taught me that the pope was Christ's vicar on earth." I told him I would pray for him. It was my last time speaking with Sebastian. A few years later, I would hear that he died tragically while hitchhiking to California, having gotten stuck sleeping on the side of the road during a freezing snowstorm. May peace be upon his gentle shade.

I then spoke with my brother Patrick. It had been a little over six months since I moved to Cincinnati, and I had begun to feel different. It is as if the initial overflow of grace I had received began to recede. I started to feel again that my father and I were different. I loved my father, and I wanted to be Catholic through and through, but I wanted independence. Speaking to my brother made my desire for this independence even stronger. Patrick said to me, "I think you converted so dad would pay for your schooling." It was the only way my conversion made sense to him—out of self-interest. I knew this was not true: I knew in my heart I converted *in spite of* my father, not because of him. But I felt I needed independence now to show that I was my own person.

Around this time, my father, being an avid reader of Thomas A. Kempis's fifteenth century work, *The Imitation of Christ*, gave me a copy to read. But I could not understand it. It felt foreign to me. The central message was withdrawal from the world and contempt for the richness of God's creation. It was the same as that St. Anthony painting in our home growing up. I didn't want to withdraw from the world. The world had led me to Jesus. I loved my father, but I was not him. In converting I had finally understood that the truth itself was much more profound than any one person who possessed it. Yes, he had the truth in Catholicism, but his particular way of internalizing it was very different than my own. I still had a great love for the natural world and all that was in it.

For years I ran and rambled all over the country and now a few foreign countries, too. I loved travel, and I loved the world. My faith felt entirely grounded in nature and the earth. Feeling my independence as a Catholic, I bought a large wall-size map to dream about places in the world I wanted to see. Those feelings of adventure and seeing the world had lain dormant since my conversion, but they had not been routed out of me. I hung my bronze crucifix over my map and wrote:

> *Now, O Lord, you hang on the cross over my map of the world.*
> *The precious blood pouring down from your wounds,*
> *Mixing with the oceans and coming ashore on the coastlines of the world.*
> *O Lord, as your blood pours down on the earth, let it not be in vain.*
> *Cultivate the planet's soil to receive you,*
> *So that your blood and water seeps into the ground nourishing her.*
> *Let my own heart be not as tightly-packed hard terrain,*
> *But as tilled soil, so that your blood can saturate my inmost being.*

O Lord, cultivate my heart to receive you, feeding my soul to salvation.

Because of my new desire for independence and because of convenience, I decided to move out of my father's house and into an apartment near the UC campus. It was a typical three-story row house often seen there—narrow, deep, and tall. An attractive young woman lived on the second floor and I on the third. To get to my apartment, I had to climb an outdoor stairwell and then enter her kitchen where an indoor stairway led to my door. Essentially, I had a key to her apartment as entering her kitchen was the only way to get to mine. When I would go home to study, I would try to quickly and quietly go through her kitchen to get upstairs. But she would often stop me to talk. I would try to excuse myself since I felt strongly tempted by her, as she was stunning, single, and my age.

Once upstairs, I would begin studying. However, my desk faced an outdoor window, the view looking directly down onto her second-floor private sundeck. Sometimes she lay tanning there under the sun, having taken off her top and bra, revealing her ravishing breasts in the bright sun. I wanted her.

I sat down and wrote a prayer, begging for help:

Blessed Virgin, I turn to you,
As the most loving beautiful woman ever to be,
And I ask you to help me stay chaste.
How much I want to sin!
Horrid, wretched, despised sin!
The murky bowels of the earth rattle and clang the iron bells,
So loud they blow my eardrums and shake my body.
My head begins to crack.
Such is the voice of sin, the call of Satan, the wretched ways
* of hell.*
Help me live my vocation, Lord—what I was made for: to
* love you.*
Keep me from Satan's dismal myrrh,
It smells sweet but is bitter to death and damnation.
Stay near me, Lord; help me be patient and prudent.

Help me not jump around, like to some harlot's bed.
Thank you, Lord, for humbling me so that I may learn to do
  your will.
I praise your name when I am in so much pain.
No, I scream, rejoicing in your name.
So much I want to stay pure.
All of this desire for goodness comes from you,
Please accept it, and give grace to other souls to come to you.

In this lustful state, I couldn't survive long. I had to move quickly before I fell. I knew very well the story of Bathsheba and King David (the Bible's psalmist). I knew my weaknesses were the same as his. The only way to avoid sin was if I left that apartment.

I wanted to be a Catholic for life. I feared my weaknesses would lead me away from Christianity. I wanted the intellectual tools to remain. So, I moved back in with my father. He understood well my problem with women and did not judge me for this. I had to decide what to do next as I had to live in the world. I couldn't just live with him forever, but for now, I would have to.

Back home, Scott Hahn's audio tapes continued to teach me about Catholicism. In some of his early recordings, he would mention that true Catholic education was lacking all over the country—that the significant Catholic universities had watered down Catholicism, but there was one school that excited him: Christendom College in Virginia. He said it was the only college teaching liberal arts from an authentic and orthodox Catholic perspective.[27]

I decided to apply to Christendom College as a transfer student. I thought being in a community of believers would give me more protection from my past sinful habits, and I would obtain more intellectual insights to live out my faith with strength. Moreover, I felt that many of my classes (history and literature) at UC were downright anti-Catholic, and I wanted to learn the truth about my faith and history. I waited to hear if I would be accepted.

As the spring of 1992 began, I was proud that I had remained a faithful Christian an entire year. As a child, I only remembered Christmas mass and being dragged to church on Sundays. But now I was walking on the narrow path of righteousness. I would hold my head high. Everywhere, I would see the cross—on churches but also on light poles and ship masts. Every time I saw a cross, I would remember whom I followed.

I was attending mass often and receiving frequent communion. I would write of those early masses: "I receive your divinity. I receive a piece of God made man. I go to your house, and I kiss the cross. I am inside you, and you are inside me." I felt incredulous when Fr. Huber explained to me that every time we partake in communion, we are participants in Christ's Last Supper. At times, I thought how out of hand it all seemed. It was beautiful but sometimes felt absurd. I asked God for light to understand what at times seemed irrational and nonsensical.

Easter Vigil finally arrived, and it was time for my confirmation at St. Peter in Chains Cathedral. It was a beautiful night; Bishop Pilarczyk of Cincinnati presided over the ceremony.[28]

The lights were all turned off as we entered the church, packed with hundreds, if not thousands, of onlookers. Only hundreds of candles lit the massive cathedral, as lectors read the entire salvation history up to Christ's resurrection. Several full-adult converts first obtained baptism before the rest of us were confirmed. Eventually, I was called up with my father behind me as sponsor. As I entered the sanctuary, Bishop Pilarczyk asked, "What confirmation name would you like to take?" I declared, "Simon-Peter."

This reflected a dualism. The authority of Peter and the succession of the popes was the primary argument that convinced me to become a Catholic. Therefore, I wanted the name Peter. But I also wanted the name Simon, to remind me of my weakness, as it was he that rejected Jesus three times (when the cock crew). I was no better than he. I wanted my confirmation name to reflect both my weakness and the Lord's strength (his rock).

Then the bishop christened my forehead with holy oil, confirming me. I was now fully accepted into the Catholic Church. It was a proud and spiritual moment for me, and it was a proud moment for my father. Even though I knew he and I were different, he loved me without condition, even when I put so many conditions on him. He was there for me now, as he had been so many times before, having given me so many second chances. He had hoped without hope, once thinking I was completely lost forever. Yet there I stood—the wild druggie, artistic hippie, and now a Catholic.

53. Christendom College

I soon got word that I was accepted into Christendom College. They agreed to take many of my UC credits so I could graduate in three years if I went to summer school twice. I started in the summer of 1992 and would finish in May of 1995.

Initially, I was concerned about it only granting liberal arts degrees. There was no journalism, geography, or any sort of practical course of study—essentially a neo-classical education. There was a core curriculum that all students must study, which included three years of philosophy, theology, history, and literature. After this, one was free to choose among those four areas to specialize in or could choose just one other area—political science and economics. My primary purpose in going to Christendom was to get this core formation, and I chose politics and economics as my major to give me at least a bit of practicality.

The school had a refutation to the critique of its core being too general and unuseful by citing John Henry Newman's treatise *The Idea of a University*. Newman sees the study of classical liberal arts as an end in itself. Knowledge is to be sought for the enlargement of the mind, which eventually leads a student to become an intellectual, providing him with wisdom, balance, and tranquility.

I liked this idea. I wanted to broaden my mind in the truth about life and the world. And I hoped that I would learn my faith well enough to withstand the temptation to abandon it when life became difficult. This fear of abandoning my faith stemmed mostly from my mother, who left her Catholic faith ten years after her conversion. I took heart in the Gospel of Mark: "Other seed fell into good soil and brought forth grain, growing up and increasing and yielding thirty and sixty and a hundredfold" (Mark 4:8). I wanted education to be the soil to nourish my faith.

I had many ups and downs at Christendom. Many of the students and faculty had the same sense of *contemptus mundi* I perceived in my father and the writings of Thomas A. Kempis. But there was a fresh spirit there, led by the new President Dr. Timothy O'Donnell, that loved and embraced the world and all that was within it. Dr. O'Donnell's theology classes were like attending seminars given by the Holy Spirit himself; the richness that filled the walls of the classroom was palpable. Attending his class was like eating a sumptuous rich steak and drinking luscious red wine. It was a spiritual feast.

Despite the difficulties I had with the older ultra-conservative remnant at the school, the curriculum and my extra reading gave me exactly what I had wanted: a well-rounded education steeped in rational truth, logic, philosophy, and the history of the faith.

Christendom College helped strengthen and nourish my faith. The veil that once propelled me to make a wager for Jesus had opened a little, allowing me to now peek at what lies in that great void of space and time, and in our own soul too: God's love.

54. The Natural Law & Industrialization

As I began my courses, I was interested in the study of natural law since I believed I had found God in nature. I had begun philosophizing as a marijuana-smoking youth, sitting under the tall trees in Roanoke's Evergreen Cemetery. I had imagined how the first seed of the first tree came into existence, which led me to a Creator, which then led me to ponder the nature and end of things on earth. I sought to know the truth of nature. Now, at Christendom, I was learning of many great philosophers who had also sought the truth through the observance of nature, one of the first being Aristotle. I learned, too, of the Roman orator Cicero, who was among the first to use the term *natural law*.[29]

During my time at Christendom, Pope St. John Paul II was regularly writing and publishing various documents. I was pleased to read *Evangelium Vitae*, where he wrote that every man and woman could discover the Creator written in their very nature, even when sin clouds their heart.[30] Often people say that God does not call one living in sin. Yet, God called me amidst great sin by revealing himself to me in his works of creation.

As an Earth Firster and organic growing hippie, I had learned to trust in my reason to understand creation. I trusted in the way things are and work, how man works, how the planet works, and how animals work. I had understood natural law from the simple observation of creation. Again, as Pope St. John Paul II would write in *Veritatis Splendor*: ". . . the natural law 'is nothing other than the light of understanding infused in us by God.'"[31]

Even though as a Christian I was no longer a hippie, I definitely still believed that man had laid waste to much of the planet through overdevelopment and industrialization. I still believed in growing and consuming organics whenever possible. Yet I was no longer dogmatic about it. I would read in Genesis, "Be fruitful and multiply, and fill the earth and subdue it; and have dominion over the fish of the sea and over the birds of the air and over every living thing that moves upon the earth" (Genesis 1:28). I now understood that God wanted man to develop the earth; therefore, industrialization no longer seemed the great evil I once thought it to be.

Wanting to clarify, I now believe that the use of chemicals and technology can properly assist nature, when appropriate. In fact, the advances in medical and industrial technology can be seen as a gift from God. I am not opposed to the use of all chemicals and products in the modification of nature. Nor am I opposed to the industrialization of society (even though I strongly prefer towns and cities where there is bountiful nature nearby). But I still do believe that pure nature should be the starting point for man to understand himself and his Creator. Chemicals and modern industrialization can often mask this understanding of man's true purpose and role in the universe. In this way, I suppose I could still be called a hippie. It also concerns me that so many in the world today do not know nature, being born and raised in the midst of cities, where there is no wildlife and no stars to wonder at. But I trust God has his own way of calling those as he found a way to call me.[32]

I do find it paradoxical that the Catholic Church teaches it wrong to use chemicals and technology to prevent pregnancy, where the alternative, ordinarily chemical-free hippies have mostly given up on this battle, and are willing to use chemicals and plastics to prevent birth. The Catholic Church is indeed the guardian of pure nature in the world today, at least in this aspect.

55. Drugs & Mysticism

At Christendom, I split my free time between landscaping on the grounds maintenance crew and reading in the tiny Christendom library. While in the library, I discovered a little book entitled *A Turning Point for Europe* by Cardinal Ratzinger (who later became Pope Benedict XVI).[33] In just a few paragraphs, he helped me understand why as a youth I had turned to drugs, as so many do. He explains why he believes modern Europe has a drug problem today (the same analysis is easily applied to the rest of the world). He begins by asking the question of why was there no large-scale drug problem in the Middle Ages since back then poppy seed was readily available. He answers this question by suggesting that in those times, spirituality filled the void of existence. Transcendence of the soul and mind existed in the Middle Ages because of their deep faith. Drugs were unnecessary. Today, because of the lack of belief in a Creator and the current philosophies of nihilism and Darwinism, there is an emptiness of the soul that seeks fulfillment in drugs.

A few years after my conversion, I would return to Europe and see the 450-year-old Bernini sculpture, the *Ecstasy of Saint Teresa,* located in the Vatican. When looking at it, I could not help but remember the words of Cardinal Ratzinger. St. Teresa was a holy woman, who—without the use of drugs—had come so close to the divine through asceticism and mysticism, that in Bernini's sculpture she appeared to be in a state of ecstasy—in what the secular world today would describe as a sexual trance. Today, many describe religious people as stiffs, but here was a work of art that showed just the opposite: a fire of love that led to sublime euphoria.

I now believe that this desire for ecstasy has led many to use drugs and alcohol (as well as use sex). This desire was a key motivation for me as a youth. I wanted to reach this state of rapture but not through the divine as interpreted by a church. I tried to reach it quickly through drugs. By my use of LSD, I felt I had come close to this state at times, yet I lacked control of my faculties. With marijuana, I thought I was broadening my mind, opening it to the universe, but it would only work when smoking and, as a side effect, would dampen my senses. Slowly, I began to seek this divine ecstasy intellectually and spiritually, which is what led me to God. I wanted to know what the created body and mind were capable of without external stimuli.

I believe that drug addicts and alcoholics are in fact dreamers. They don't accept the world as it is. Instead, they feel it is unjust and brutal—sometimes because of the family they were born into or other circumstances that have befallen them. In a way, they are correct to see the injustice in life. In one sense they are like the dreamer Don Quixote. Yet their way of solving their problems only makes their own circumstances worse since drugs have such a disastrous consequence on the human body. Even so, one cannot take away their idealism. The world needs more dreamers—but dreamers who have their full capacity; only these can change the injustice they see and bring forward a more beautiful world.

I recently returned to Ithaca in research for this book and went to Aron's house in the hope that I could find out what happened to him and the organic bakery, having lost touch with him long ago. He no longer lived there, but the current resident happily invited me in. She reminded me of the allure of Ithaca from my days past: a friendly, open-minded, earthy, deeply spiritual, thoughtful, and attractive person. She too had worked—rather managed—a local organic farm for many years. But she was taking time off to pursue a spiritual quest and was using the home as a sort of mini-retreat while she studied eastern philosophical and spiritual thought. She told me, "In my quest, I have recently learned that *all pain is either anticipated or remembered.*" She told me, "I have begun to learn how to transcend pain by living without a past or future—only in the eternal now."

In a way, this could be seen as another remedy to the drug problem but from an eastern perspective. Drugs are an escape from a reality that is often one of deep pain. Drugs ease the pain for a few moments. The difference for the Christian is that we do not free ourselves from all pain through existential enlightenment, but instead we accept the pain of our past, present, and future and offer it as a sacrifice to our Creator. Thus, in eastern thought it appears that detachment from the world can help heal our problems; but for Christians, it is instead an attachment to God—a mysticism based on love of another and a desire to be united to him in eternity.

However, one addresses the drug problem, this understanding of its origins can be helpful in remedying it.

56. Dante & Beatrice

My favorite classes at Christendom were English literature, and my favorite book was the entire three parts of Dante Alighieri's *Divine Comedy*, a classic dated to the fourteenth century. The part most moving to me was not all the terrible punishments meted out by the devil, or all the various creative purifying methods of purgatory, nor the high levels of heaven; it was instead a woman, Beatrice, whom Dante met at the beginning of his journey and who would later guide him into paradise. Our professor explained that Beatrice was a symbol of—or a way to—the Beatific Vision, this vision being God in his pure radiant essence—complete beauty and grace.

I like to dream of this Beatific Vision as the most radiant and beautiful phenomena I will ever see. I believe Dante was making the point that Beatrice, the beauty of an ideal woman, was the closest a man could get to this eternal vision. I agree. The grace and mystery of the feminine form is the most awe-inspiring element of the universe—the effect it has on the eyes as well as the heart and senses. The beauty of the natural wild earth is a close second.

Thus, all of the radiant beauty on earth will be as only a reflection of what awaits us in heaven.

I recently read that Beatrice was a real person whom Dante fell madly in love with and remained so his entire life. Her real name is thought to be Beatrice di Folco Portinari. Her beauty and grace so inspired Dante that after her death at just twenty-four years he began an intense composition of poems in awe and in honor of her, eventually producing them under the title *La Vita Nuova*. His love was platonic as both of them barely knew each other, but from the moment he saw her, she remained in his heart until death: "From the first day I beheld her face in this life . . . I've never ceased from following her song."[34]

This is a truly poetic way to understand love: that I can love another madly, even though I cannot be a part of her life. My entire life had been one of fascination with women, beauty, and love. I had always needed a woman's charms, her fragrance, her mystery, and her sexuality. It was a form of worship and obsession. As a young child, I was enamored with beauty and the feminine model, even to the extent of it affecting my gender identity. And as I grew up, I had an obsession of always needing a woman to be with sexually and emotionally. Finally, as I grew toward my faith, I still needed to possess the pure beauty I had encountered in the stories of *Don Quixote* and in the veiled, mysterious Esther from Germany.

I often think I could have channeled my own love of the feminine into homosexuality. I have never had overtly sexual attraction to men, but I can recognize a handsome man. Perhaps these thoughts could have been confused for physical attraction if I had not been such a natural philosopher, questioning nature as a youth. I saw God in nature early on and slowly was led to believe in a certain self-taught natural law. What are the purposes of things, the purpose of sex, and the purpose of attraction? Had I not been so dogmatic on asking the why of everything, perhaps I would not believe what I do now.

Homosexuality, like heterosexuality and all sexual desire, is, in essence, a desire of love, a desire of wanting something greater than oneself, a desire for style and fashion as well as human affection, and even a desire for God. Yet, in fallen man, there is often considerable confusion between the love of *phileo* (brother) and that of *eros* (erotic). This love and desire can be corrupted into illicit sexual preferences and eventually to ideology, the moral right to have certain sexual relations. Moreover, it can also turn into an addictive drug; the heightened sensation of sex can become irresistible when the brain begins to rely on the strong chemicals released in it during sex. When sex is not paired to monogamy and marriage, it can degrade the love of neighbor we are naturally born with into utility, the using of another for our own pleasure.

In this age, when our entire culture has become confused by sexuality and gender identity, it is heartening for me to remember that, according to Catholic thought, God is neither male nor female but, instead, has both characteristics in complete form.[35] There will be no gender in heaven, there will be no sexuality in heaven, there will be no marriage, there will be no drugs, and there will be no attachments to alcohol or music. There will not even be religion. There will just be love—the most intense light of beauty that will fill our souls with the greatest pleasure, that of pure joy.

Now, with the help of Dante, I understand that love can transcend time and place. Love is not only physical touch and the sensation of presence as I so often had thought of it and had abused it. It is and can be, much higher and more profound if sanctified in this vision. In fact, this type of love does not even need reality—much like Don Quixote's Dulcinea: she was an old country wench, but he saw her as magnificence itself, and his feelings of love for her drove him to desire nobility and to help those in need. I believe that this *feeling* of love is (in part) for ourselves, even though we project it onto another person. God made us to seek love and to cherish this feeling, perhaps because his nature is love itself and he made us in his likeness. This understanding is comforting since I can now understand my sentiments are noble, even when human love is unrequited or fails.

This glimpse into beatific love was not something I fully understood at Christendom. The idea of it was planted in my mind reading Dante. But it took another twenty years for this seedling to actually grow into a tree.

I have been blessed to receive much good spiritual direction over these past twenty-five years as a Christian. Yet I have learned that some advice, while applicable to most, not always fits me.[36] For example, I have been told that when I see a beautiful woman, I should divert my eyes so as not to fall into sin. And another maxim is that when I see a lovely woman, I should think of her as my mother or sister so as to respect her. While this is true and good advice, I find it incomplete for me. Motherly and sisterly love is meant to be platonic and will not necessarily inspire the great and noble acts of a man as will passion for a woman. Don Quixote needed Dulcinea, not his mother or sister, to ennoble what he believed were great acts for God. Dante needed the magnificent Beatrice to inspire his vision of heaven. Sometimes great beauty, in and of itself, can and should influence the higher passions of man. Thus, it's a fine point of distinction as it is easy to illicitly lust after a gorgeous woman, but if one can transform that passion into divine inspiration, much better.

Thoughtful artists in the world may understand this point and take heart in these words. For example, the deeply devout Catholic Michelangelo may have lived with monk-like chastity while still writing erotically styled sonnets (some even referring to men) and producing some of the most magnificent art ever known to man.[37] Would the advice of covering the eyes have worked for Michelangelo while he crafted some of the most significant art in history?

All of this helps me to understand that beauty can be of assistance to the divine, even though one cannot fully obtain it in life.[38] In my case, I have never been married, despite my desire and plans to the contrary, and this once created in me a sense of frustrated purpose. But now, I happily accept that there may be no one able to fulfill my deepest yearnings for true love on this planet. My heart may await to see this grandeur in the next life, using only the fading memories of love to guide my way. But I rest in the magnificent eternal vision of my Beatrice, standing above, bidding me join her.

> O Lady, thou in whom my hope is strong . . .
> From slavery to freedom thou hast drawn me in every way,
> and over every path . . .
> And she, though so far off she seemed, looked down at me and
> smiled;
> Then to the Eternal Fount she turned again.[39]

57. Graduation

A few months before graduation from Christendom, I was to see Esther again. She had married a professor from Germany, who had recently been assigned to a six-month post at a university in Ohio. I was invited to visit her and her new family (she had a child now). I met them during a break from school. I had loved her once, but the romantic love was gone now, and I was satisfied in that. In fact, I wasn't sure if I ever truly loved her; perhaps I had only profoundly admired her and was eternally grateful for her role in my conversion.

Still, I was nervous as I went to the front door. When she opened the door of her home to greet me, instead of happiness at seeing her again, I felt deeply saddened. Her angelic face was now blank-white and sour. Her smile was gone, in its place a permanent frown, and her face and arms appeared to have bruises on them. She invited me inside where I met her husband (who was very tall) and the newborn child (who was loudly crying). We all sat down for dinner, a very simple bread and soup.

I felt odd being there, thinking her husband may feel jealous of me. Perhaps he would want to know details about my and Esther's past. But instead, he only wanted to talk about religion and dogma. From the moment I sat down, he started to preach about true Christianity and the evils of Catholicism, warning me that the pope was the Antichrist leading the world astray. He, too, had no smile on his face nor did he have charisma. He was even more severe than Esther's father, who would preach against the papists on a soapbox in front of the Catholic Minster Cathedral in Freiburg.

I had already heard this before. I just listened. I hadn't come to try to convert anyone this time. At some point during the past years, I realized I had no desire to try to convince anyone of my beliefs. I loved freedom for myself and others, and I hated all forms of peer pressure. That is not to say I wasn't apostolic, but for me, the best way to convince another is by letting them find their own way. I believe one must decide according to their own conscience in total freedom. I only help with small nudges and when asked.

Esther barely spoke; instead, she sort-of cowered. Her child was unhappy as well. I wondered to myself if this man was physically abusing her and possibly the child. The style and grace I had remembered were now breathless and inanimate.

The dinner felt as if it ended abruptly. I wanted to go, and I could feel her husband wanted me to go as well. The tension was palpable. I have never seen or heard from her again in over twenty years. I pray that she is today safe and happy. From my heart, I thank her, that pure and mysterious snowflake at the Freiburg Minster, for having been willing to speak to me, a grungy Earth First! hippie, and for having dared to help me purify my life for God. I hope to see her in the life to come.

I graduated on a bright, cool, fresh day in May of 1995, a very proud moment. Almost all of my siblings came to the graduation. They didn't need to come. None of them believed what I believed in. None of them had ever graduated from college, and they were far away from religion or any organized spirituality (except Russell who had begun to attend mass on Sundays). Yet, I am eternally thankful they did come. They were proud that I was graduating from college, even if it was from a profoundly Catholic school with which they disagreed. They stepped out of themselves and made this long trip just for me. An act of selflessness—they had no obligation.

My mother was not there as she had died exactly one year before, following a bout with cancer. After my conversion, I began to pray that she would come back to her Catholic or Christian faith before her death. I was overjoyed to receive a letter from her a few months before she died, stating that she had begun to attend a Christian church and to pray every day. She wrote: "I do believe this illness has brought me closer to God. I feel his presence in my life every day. . . . Suffering does bring out strength." She had also begun to read books by Corrie Ten Boom, a devout Christian Dutch woman, who helped many Jews escape the Nazi Holocaust during World War II. In the early hours of May 5, 1994, she lost her fight and was called home. She was fifty-four years old.

I attempted to see her during her final days on earth, but I arrived just hours after she had passed. I visited her at the morgue. I wanted to be alone. It was a cold, sanitized room with a tiled, hard floor. She lay on a stretcher in the center of the room. I looked at her body lying there, elevated about four feet, draped in white. Her hands were cold. Her face was pale. Her spirit was gone.

I wept uncontrollably, falling to the floor. All my newly budding intellectualism was as nothing in the face of pure love for her. I missed her immediately and was thankful for all she had given me. I was happy to have shown her that I was no longer the lousy son I had been for so many years. As a youth, I had stolen from her, lied to her repeatedly, and caused her pain and frustration by my continued use of drugs and alcohol, and yet she proceeded to give me many fresh starts. I would abuse her love over and over again, despite her giving me near total freedom to be myself. But finally, she had seen the new me and was happy with me. She was proud of me.

I prayed to an all-powerful and merciful God that he would grant her a path to him:

> *Please, Lord, do not look at her sins;*
> *Look only at the good she has done.*
> *You alone know the deepest recesses of her heart;*
> *Only you can see her purity and goodness.*
> *Help me be better in my own life;*
> *Let my life reflect her love for you.*
> *Grant her eternal rest and peace in your bosom.*

She would have physically been at my graduation had she been alive. But I knew that she was with me in spirit.

Of course, my father was at my graduation. I have been hard on him my entire life; I can be a churlish son. During my time at Christendom, as I got to know other Catholic couples and families—strong men and women that remained together, my fallen nature began to compare him to them. That initial grace of forgetfulness had gone, and now my grievances were endless. Why did he file the divorce papers? Why did he get an annulment instead of enduring it? Why didn't he encourage me to seriously pursue a profession instead of just talking about saints and priests? Why couldn't he be more successful? He is the reason I am so strange and different than everyone else. He is the reason I will never be successful. My envious and judgmental mind would go on with these endless internal complaints.

Yet, anyone can easily see my father's great love for me; it was nearly boundless. He tried to help me when I first got involved in drugs. Yet I ran.

Each time I hoped to get on the right course, he would give me a new chance, always giving me the benefit of his love, even as I continued to drop out of school and run away. I do believe he made a mistake putting me in Straight. But I can only forgive and try to understand. In fact, he did not know about all the abuse and cultish activity at Straight. He has recently apologized to me after learning about it, following my research and refreshed recollection of what happened.

Yes, he was always focused on religion and had a traditional view of contempt for the world. This always bothered me, but I must be loving and understanding. He was born in a different age and grew up with certain traditions. He is as much a product of his time as am I. And now, I too am very focused on religion—much unlike in my youth. So, we have that in common now. And I must be clear: he has always loved the beauty of creation, and his traditionalist view of contempt for the world has sharply modified with time— now understanding the concept of *passionately loving the world*.[40] Even as an old man, he has grown in his faith. Today he is living the life of a modern hermit, alone at night with his prayer books and images, yet during the day he works hard in the world, despite his octogenarian age, to effectuate the faith and the truth of man by devoting long hours every day to helping the pro-life movement.

I have recently seen pictures of my father as a young man. It struck me that I had never seen him as a youth (as my first awareness of him was in his forties). The picture shows a wide smile, broad shoulders, muscular frame, straight back, fashionably dressed, and exuding confidence. My consciousness of my father started as a five-year-old at a time when he was descending into a sort of *purgatorio*: a wife self-medicating and attempting suicide, a broken marriage, and wild runaway children. God sometimes allows such extreme suffering that it can bend the backbone of a man. But as Job was always faithful, so was my father, and for that I am thankful.

God may not have given me a wealthy and successful man of the world as a father. But he did give me all that is genuinely needed. He was the one to plant that first seed of faith into my heart. Had that seed not been planted, no tree would have grown. Yes, we are different, but the one thing we hold in common is our love and assent to the Catholic Church. And this is an essential part of both of our lives. St. Teresa of Calcutta is well-known for saying, "God does not require that we be successful, only that we be faithful."

Perhaps he should have been a priest instead of marrying my mother, but this was not God's plan. Because of this change in his vocation, I was born. And I was born for some reason, perhaps not even known to me yet.

I will never forget a prayer my father taught me as a new Catholic:

> God has created me to do Him some definite service. He has committed some work to me which He has not committed to another. I have my mission. I may never know it in this life, but I shall be told it in the next. I am a link in a chain, a bond of connection between persons. He has not created me for naught. I shall do good; I shall do His work. I shall be an angel of peace, a preacher of truth in my own place, while not intending it if I do but keep His commandments. Therefore, I will trust Him, whatever or wherever I am, I can never be thrown away. If I am in sickness, my sickness may serve Him, in perplexity, my perplexity may serve Him. If I am in sorrow, my sorrow may serve Him. He does nothing in vain. He knows what He is about. He may take away my friends. He may throw me among strangers. He may make me feel desolate, make my spirits sink, hide my future from me. Still, He knows what He is about.[41]

I have to wonder, reading this prayer now, if God allowed so much to happen both to my own father and to me so that I could eventually write this book for the benefit of others.

Just a few months before my graduation, I met Fr. John Hardon at Christendom. He died in 2000, and his cause for canonization was opened in 2005. He was an American Jesuit, a writer and theologian, who worked extensively with St. Teresa of Calcutta and collaborated with Cardinal Ratzinger on the *Catechism of the Catholic Church*.

I was his chauffeur from the airport to Christendom, where he gave a lecture. I told him about my life, and we prayed together. He encouraged me to write every day and to eventually tell my story saying, "It's important that your experiences be known (what God has done for you)." He promised to pray for me. Saying farewell, he said, "God has plans for you." I hope that Fr. Hardon is looking down now to spread this little book into the hands of those who need it: the ramblers, alternative truth seekers, drug addicts, kids from broken homes, those with mental problems or gender identity issues, those called the losers in life, and those who have no problems but want reasons for the hope they have.

58. Rambling

Today, in churches I attend, and in books I read, the parable of the Prodigal Son is almost always told in the same way (*see* Luke 15:11–32). The story goes that there is a loving father and two sons. One son goes away and wastes his father's inheritance, and the other stays home working. The son that left hits bottom and finally returns home. His loving father then showers him with gifts and even kills the fatted calf for him because he came back home. The parable's lesson is that God is always willing to forgive our waywardness when we humbly ask his help.

While I know the following may not be entirely correct, I find this alternative understanding an enlightening way to reflect on it: perhaps the father is praising the prodigal son for having taken a risk, having gone out into the world to find his own way, even if he finally realizes he has failed and needs help. The good son, who never left, never took a risk, is bitter: *Where is my fatted calf?* Perhaps God is telling us he wants us to go out, take a risk, and see the vast created world, even get down and dirty with the pigs sometimes, so that we can see him with greater love and without bitterness.

Of course, God never desires that men sin, but it is not a sin to see the world, to experience working on a pig farm, or to use all our money in crazy pursuits. This is not the way most people want to hear this parable, instead being accustomed more to the phrase: *be a good boy and do as you are told.*

In closing, dear reader (who I profoundly thank for having read my book), I would like to extol the *virtue* of rambling: of travel, of wanderlust. As a child, my little mind saw in a sort of vision that I would one day *see the world*. I then broke out as a runaway, hitchhiking to Florida. Later this desire morphed into a wondering about from state to state and country to country, without purpose or plan. Finally, in the present, it has become well-thought-out, planned trips to see more of what I love: the world.

But generally, all of these ramblings are connected with this one great adventurous idea: exploration and travel. Much can be learned of the world in books and stories, but the random beauty of life pours upon us when we actually enter a place. Real beauty is in hearing the voices of others and in our eyes capturing real-time images—all during wanderings upon earth.

I believe that travel is necessary for a person to fully develop their mind, expand their knowledge of the world, and even to find God himself. But this is not a new idea. Richard Lassels, a Catholic priest and travel writer from the early seventeenth century, is known for his book *A Complete Journey through Italy*. In it, he argues that any serious student of the arts and history must travel. He suggested that all "young lords" make a "Grand Tour" (a trip through Europe) in their life, to truly understand the realities of the world of politics, art, society, and economy. Anyone who has traveled knows this instinctively, including the great Catholic author Hillaire Belloc, who made such a Grand Tour by foot and who wrote a book entitled *The Path to Rome,* which was first published in 1902 and is still in print today.

I feel blessed that God infused this idea of travel in me when I was very young. I didn't conceive the idea to *see the world;* it just was. Today, even though I work as an attorney, I have been blessed to have been to nearly one hundred countries and territories and am able to work during many of my travels in making documentary educational videos for a non-profit I founded, inspired by my life's progenitor, that foolish gentleman Don Quixote. Travel has been the most important part of my life. I often think it has helped me to stay away from drugs and other bad influences. It is exciting and refreshing to see the world. It excites the soul and heart, keeping one's spirit alive and full of happiness without the need for substances. I recommend travel wholeheartedly to anyone with similar problems today. There is a sense of awe and wonder that it imparts.

In the years following my conversion, I began to lose my way. I slowly transformed from a wild-hearted adventurer to a domesticated lawyer seeking to emulate the life of St. Thomas More. I had then thought my rambling youth had just been a phase, and now it was time for me to work hard as a professional, find a young woman, settle down, and live the domesticated life. But I had pigeon-holed my conception of the good: the influential profession, the beautiful wife, the children, the car, the fancy home. All these things are good but can entangle and confuse some with hearts for the wild world.

Dear reader, it's important to let your heart soar and, if need be, blow up the preconceived notion of yourself or of what is a good life. The good life comes when you accept yourself as you are and make positive whatever comes your way. You don't have to be that saint you venerate or that person you think others want you to be. Perhaps a log cabin in the woods is better than a big home with a mortgage, and an old pickup is better than a smooth-riding Mercedes. With the money and time saved, you can write that book you always wanted to write, or make that trip to the Acropolis, or swim in the same waters as the shipwrecked St. Paul. Perhaps, at least for some, the good life is to see all that God has created . . . while letting one's heart soar above the masses in an ethereal dream of walking with the Creator.

I had turned from a pot smoking, hitchhiking rambler to a conservative Catholic, and then I swung back again (at least in my mind) to try to find my true self. After nearly fifty years on the planet, I think I can finally say I have found him, and, in fact, I like him, even if he is not what I had always wanted or expected. I am not that winning (but often morally stressed) attorney who turns to gold all that he touches. I'd rather have my head in the clouds breathing the free misty air God has blown across this great earth. I am a dreamer and will die a dreamer, even if my dreams are all fool's errands. My actions and intentions in life are done with love for that one great Being of all.

Today, as I look back at all of my travels and misadventures, I believe that God himself was guiding me, even pushing me. He knew that I would eventually find him in all of his grandeur, despite my having rolled around with the pigs for a while.

I meditated on nature's God on Roanoke's Old Solitude Farm.
I rode a Greyhound through wild, wonderful West Virginia after a thrilling escape.
I saw the beauty of the raw desert along the Rio Grande.
I felt tragedy and isolation in the giant redwoods of Santa Cruz.
I experienced imprisonment in Florida and total despair and loneliness in Nebraska.
I rode free through the wild forests and lakes of the Upper Peninsula.
I learned the ways of nature through organic farming in Ithaca.
I was the recipient of a real miracle in Germany.
I felt the purity and happiness of platonic love in Madrid.

All of these travels appeared at the time to be a series of ramblings through life with no apparent points of connectedness or purpose. Yet somehow God was a small voice in each of these places, whispering in the wind and rain to my unworthy soul. In each new place, there was a memory conceived in my mind, and each memory helped me grow closer and closer to him.

Had I not gone outside, took the risk of adventure, and wondered at the splendor of the earth, perhaps I would have died long ago by a drug overdose inside some psychiatric ward. I give thanks to God for travel, for my rambling spirit.

Alexandr Solzhenitsyn once said, when acknowledging what had brought him from communist atheism to faith in God, *Bless you prison!*[42]

And so in like sentiment, I declare:

Bless you rambling!

Endnotes

---

[1] Aristotle, *Nicomachean Ethics: Politics*, Book VIII, Chapters 5–7 (B.C. 384–322).

[2] Id.

[3] The Venerable Matt Talbot, an alcoholic who is now considered for sainthood, could be seen as a real-life incarnation of this ideal.

[4] My father never beat his children. He used the belt on me once and slapped me once. This was not unusual parental behavior at the time.

[5] "Member" is not an accurate way to describe the participants of the program since the word often connotes a voluntariness, which for most was not the case. The word "subject" is more accurate in initial phases of the program, but often the youth later voluntarily remains in the program, thus making the term "member" more accurate in later phases. I use the word member here only for consistency. Those who have spent time in the program often refer to themselves as *Straightlings*.

[6] *See,* Mylo Geyelin, "Growing Straight, Inc. Remains Controversial," *St. Petersburg Times*, July 6, 1981 (cited in Wikipedia entry for "Straight, Incorporated", pulled on November 27, 2017).

[7] The pier was torn down in 2016.

[8] *See,* Louis Aguilar, "5 Shot Dead in Roanoke Apartment," *The Washington Post*, Jan. 2, 1995.

[9] *See,* David Reed, "Roanoke killer's fate weighed," *The Free Lance Star* [Fredericksburg, VA], August 4, 1995. *See also,* Phil Reeves, "Five deaths shatter quiet US city," *UK Independent,* Jan. 1, 1995. *See also,* photo posted at Tumblr <http://adeadlyinnocence.tumblr.com/post/130844826722/on-january-1-1995-27-year-old-robert-michael-may>, pulled on November 27, 2017.

[10] *See,* Surviving Straight Inc., website, which compiles articles and documentation pertaining to Straight <http://survivingstraightinc.com>, pulled on November 27, 2017.

[11] *See,* Radley Balko, "Drug War Casualties," *Fox News*, May 23, 2002.

[12] *See,* Drug Free America Foundation, Inc. website <https://dfaf.org/about-us/founding-members.html>, pulled on November 27, 2017.

[13] *See,* Jeff Gilmore, "Defending Environmentalists' Punching Bag: Lake Powell," James E. Rogers College of Law, University of Arizona (cited in Wikipedia article "Glen Canyon Dam", pulled on November 27, 2017).

[14] *See,* Fr. Francisco López de Gómara, *Cortés, The Life of the Conqueror,* trans. & eds. by Lesley Byrd Simpson (The Regents University of California 1964).

15 Francisco López de Gómara, *La conquista de Mexico, 1552*, John Carter Brown Library (Jan. 31, 2012), page 51. [Original Source, Francisco López de Gómara, *La conquista de Mexico, 1552* (Saragossa, Spain 1553)]. Translation of original source by C. Ramirez.

16 Id.

17 Bernal Díaz del Castillo, a Spanish conquistador who participated in the conquest of Mexico as a soldier under Hernán Cortés, wrote a book of his experiences after Gómara's, claiming Gómara minimized some of the harsher facts. *See*, Bernal Díaz del Castillo, *The True History of the Conquest of New Spain* (1576).

18 Years later I would write this couple in thanks for what they did for me. Eventually Monsieur Houlliere died, and I lost touch with Madame. I give thanks to them even today, emotionally filling my eyes with tears.

19 I did not have a debit card. Back then, tourists used traveler's checks and money wires.

20 I believe this was Dolores Ibárruri, a Spanish communist politician of Basque origin, known for her slogan *¡No Pasarán!* ("They shall not pass") used during the Spanish Civil War.

21 I do not wish to denigrate the military or those who serve, of which I now have great respect; I am only stating how I then felt.

22 Blaise Pascal, *Pensées* § 233 (c. 1670).

23 Today, now knowing more about my own character, I realize my reaction was probably also due in part to my being an introvert. I used to think I was strange for avoiding crowds, but now I understand it's just part of being an introverted person.

24 *See*, Thomas Jefferson, *The Jefferson Bible: The Life and Morals of Jesus of Nazareth Extracted* (c. 1819).

25 Geoffrey Chaucer, *Troilus and Criseyde* (c. 1380s).

26 St. Augustine of Hippo, *Confessions* (c. 400).

27 This audio tape would likely have predated his obtaining a professorship at the competing Franciscan University of Steubenville in Ohio.

28 I didn't know the bishop, thus it felt a bit impersonal. Yet this was the way the RCIA program was done, no meeting beforehand. It saddened and angered me to learn later that he was involved in scandal and crime, having plead no contest to several misdemeanor counts of failing to report felonies of sexual abuse by priests in his diocese.

29 Cicero, The Republic, II, 22. (c. 54 to 51 BC).

30 Pope St. John Paul II, "Evangelium Vitae," 29 (March 25, 1995): The Creator is "...indeed written in the heart of every man and woman, has echoed in every conscience 'from the beginning,' from the time of creation itself, in such a way that, despite the negative consequences of sin, it can also be known in its essential traits by human reason."

31 Pope St. John Paul II, "Veritatis Splendor," 40 (August 6, 1993).

32 I recently learned of, and visited, the Madonna House (a Catholic lay apostolate) in the Canadian woods. It was founded by the Servant of God Catherine de Hueck Doherty. She is a mystical spiritual writer who praises the natural world, having written such books as *Apostolic Farming* and *I Live on an Island*. Her books, written close to nature, sing of finding God in silence and solitude in our loud technological world. She speaks of the farmer who touches God himself when he works in creation.

33 Cardinal Ratzinger later became Pope Benedict XVI, and is known today as Pope Emeritus Benedict XVI. I will refer to him here as Cardinal Ratzinger for simplicity.

34 Dante Alighieri, "Paradiso," *Divine Comedy*, Canto 30, (c. 1308–1320), translated from the Latin.

35 *See*, Catechism of the Catholic Church, No. 239.

36 I do believe in the importance of spiritual direction. However, it is important to remember that my faith is solely my choice. Today, I listen to others for enlightenment in making my own decisions, not to emulate or please another. I no longer deny myself the primary responsibility of seeking God's will in my life.

37 *See*, Anthony Hughes, "Michelangelo," (Phaidon, 1997), page 326 (cited in Wikipedia entry for "Michelangelo", pulled on November 27, 2017).

38 I have recently read a letter written by Cardinal Ratzinger entitled *The Feeling of Things, Contemplation of Beauty*, which was sent to a Communion and Liberation Meeting in August of 2002. In it, Cardinal Ratzinger reflects on how beauty has such a force as to compel our hearts toward truth and transcendence.

39 Dante Alighieri, "Paradiso," *Divine Comedy*, Canto 31 (c. 1308–1320), trans. Courtney Langdon, (Cambridge Harvard University Press, 1921).

40 In 1967, a Spanish priest, St. Josemaría Escrivá, entitled a famous homily by this phrase. I find it an excellent rebuttal to the idea of *contemptus mundi*.

41 Cardinal John Henry Newman, "The Mission of My Life," *Part III, Meditations on Christian Doctrine, Hope in God—Creator* (March 6, 1848).

42 Aleksandr Solzhenitsyn, *The Gulag Archipelago 1918–1956* (Éditions du Seuil, 1973).

Made in the
USA
Middletown, DE